The
FRIENDSHIP
BOOK

of Francis Gay

D. C. THOMSON & CO., LTD.
London   Glasgow   Manchester   Dundee

A Thought

For Each Day

In 1976

Friendship is a gracious thing
Lovely as a prayer.

Edna Jaques

FROST FLOWERS

The architecture most admired
  Is that which copies Nature's face,
Though never has it quite aspired
  To such variety and grace.

DAVID HOPE

THOUGHTS

There is a unity in Nature's actions;
*   The loveliest views rejoice the thoughtful man.*
For sea and rocks and flowers are all reflections
*   Of one unfolding plan.*

DAVID HOPE

JANUARY

<u>THURSDAY—JANUARY 1.</u>

OLD is the world but new the year,
    What are you going to do
Ere 1976 grows old?
    A challenge this, to you!
A lot of lonely folk there are,
    And many sad or ill,
If you've been kind to some, why not
    Be even kinder still?
There's nothing folk need more today
Than cheer to help them on their way.

<u>FRIDAY—JANUARY 2.</u>

I READ the other day the classic story of Prince Alexis of Russia who, knowing that one day he would rule over his father's kingdom, determined to get to know his people before he came to the throne.

So he set off to tour the country, with a retinue of courtiers and soldiers to impress his future subjects. But at their appearance the people fled and hid in terror and fear.

Bitterly disappointed, Alexis consulted a wise old friend who told him he had gone about it in the wrong way. " First win their trust and love," he counselled, " and you will win their allegiance."

So the story, beloved of Russia, tells how Alexis trained to become a physician and then went humbly among the people, tending to their needs and healing them with compassion. When at last he came to the throne the people recognised their friend, and because he had won their hearts and trust, willingly gave him their loyalty.

SATURDAY—JANUARY 3.

DR MARTIN LUTHER KING, the coloured Baptist preacher who fought so courageously for the rights of American Negroes, was also known as a gentle man of peace — one of his sayings was that the " eye for an eye " policy ends up leaving everybody blind.

If only the leaders of our troubled world today would remember his words !

SUNDAY—JANUARY 4.

AND now abideth faith, hope, charity, these three; but the greatest of these is charity.

MONDAY—JANUARY 5.

CHARLES SPURGEON, the famous evangelist, was known for his wit. Often, when he was preaching, the congregation became, it is said, one vast smile.

But his wit had sometimes a sting as on the occasion when he said, " If you are Christians, smile and, if not, your ordinary faces will do."

He was asked by the vacancy committee of one church, " Can you get us a minister big enough to fill our church?" " I can't do that," said Spurgeon, " but if you fill the church I'll get you a preacher big enough to fill the pulpit."

" Your minister looks as if he needs a new suit," he twitted a congregation. " I'll give ten shillings and we'll take up a collection for the rest."

So widespread was his fame that in the Highlands of Scotland a customer would go into the village shop on a Saturday, lay down a penny and receive in return a copy of Spurgeon's weekly sermon without a word having to be spoken.

THE FRIENDSHIP BOOK

TUESDAY—JANUARY 6.

I DON'T suppose the name David Everett means very much to you. But you will be sure to recognise a couple of lines he wrote as an obscure schoolboy in eighteenth century America. The occasion was an entertainment given by his school and he was asking the audience's indulgence for not being a very good speaker. He ended his speech with the words, " Large streams from little fountains flow; tall oaks from little acorns grow."

It's just as true today.

WEDNESDAY—JANUARY 7.

P ERHAPS you fear to face a year
  Entirely on your own.
The one who walked with you has gone —
  Yet are you quite alone?
Each mile will hold a memory sweet
To strengthen you, to guide your feet.

THURSDAY—JANUARY 8.

THERE are always two ways of looking at things.

I'm reminded of this by a story I heard from Mrs Jenny Wilson, of Marchmont Road, Edinburgh. She has two children, Susan, who's eight, and Moira, five. Usually the sisters are the best of friends, but the other day Jenny overheard an argument.

It seemed to have ended in Susan's favour when she told her little sister severely, " Remember, I'm three years older than you !"

There was silence for a moment. Then up piped wee Moira.

" Well," she retorted, " you remember I'm three years newer than you !"

THE FRIENDSHIP BOOK

DID you read about the Scottish doctor who was sent home very ill with Lassa fever? Dr Kennedy, a Scot working in Nigeria, contracted this disease with no known cure and, sadly, he died.

This story brought to mind a Nigerian chief called Mandomi who, some years ago, was stricken with the dreaded sleeping sickness. Many of his tribesmen had already died, but Mandomi had heard about the great white doctors and hospitals in London and he decided to put himself at their disposal, so that by studying him they might perfect a cure. Much against his people's wishes, he set off for London, where he was immediately hospitalised. There he underwent many tests and treatments.

Eventually, however, he died, after months of infirmity. To this day, there is a plaque on the wall in the ward where he once lay. On it is his name, followed by the words : " Greater love hath no man than this."

IT was rather a busy day in our local shop, and I couldn't help overhearing some of the ladies discussing a new neighbour.

" She seems quite friendly," one voice tentatively suggested but, very quickly, a much firmer voice answered, " It's early days yet. I'm afraid I don't make friends easily."

She sounded quite proud of the fact. And it's true quite a few of us take a certain pride in being " reserved." But I wonder if we're right. I know my heart went out to the unknown newcomer and I couldn't help recalling a saying I'd once heard : " Your Friend Was Once A Stranger — So A Stranger Is A Friend."

THE FRIENDSHIP BOOK

SUNDAY—JANUARY 11.

WITH God all things are possible.

MONDAY—JANUARY 12.

THE people Mr Surly meets
Are always very grim;
And every day — so he declares —
They're most unkind to him.
I wonder if the trouble is
That Mr Surly's frown
Makes friendly people seem to him
The meanest folk in town?

TUESDAY—JANUARY 13.

IT'S easy to get hold of the wrong end of the stick.
George Irving, of Glasgow, was walking along a street near the university when he saw four young people grouped in conversation and glancing occasionally towards a collecting-box for crippled children at the entrance to a wine shop.

George had the uneasy feeling they were up to something. Their long hair and unorthodox dress only helped to make him more suspicious.

Then, as he drew nearer, he saw them take all the money they had from their pockets. They pooled it, then taking out what they needed for food, put all the rest in the collecting-box and, smiling to each other, walked away.

"I felt so utterly ashamed," George told me. "I had such unfounded suspicions about these young people. Then I saw their spontaneous generosity whilst I had already passed the box and given nothing."

At times it's nice to be proved wrong. For George Irving, that was one of them!

WEDNESDAY—JANUARY 14.

I HAVE often wondered how the clerical collar first came to be worn. Recently a friend gave me what seems to be the reason.

It appears that at one time when the monks in their habits worked in the fields they became literally " hot under the collar." So to catch the sweat that dropped from their brows they got into the custom of wearing a neckerchief, usually of white linen. These became known as " sweat rags."

In time the white circle on the habit of the monk became a common feature, and the whole distinguished the clerical dress. So the " dog collar " is not the mark, as often assumed, of an easy life but the badge of an honourable and hard-working profession.

THURSDAY—JANUARY 15.

I THOUGHT you might like to hear this story about my four-year-old friend Ian. He had been learning " All Things Bright and Beautiful " at Sunday school, and when Mum went to tuck him at night and read him his story, Ian asked if, instead of their usual prayer, they might sing the new hymn. Mum helped out with the verses and Ian finished up with the chorus we all know so well :

All things bright and beautiful, all creatures great and small,
All things wise and wonderful, the Lord God made them all.

Mum tucked in the blankets and just as she was leaving the room a wee voice said, " That was a shame for God, wasn't it, Mummy ?"

" What do you mean, Ian ?" she asked.

And Ian explained, " Nobody helped Him."

THE FRIENDSHIP BOOK

THE Boys' Brigade may not be so popular as it was, but it certainly gives a boy a pride in himself.

An example of this is of the days when the annual parade and inspection of the Glasgow battalion was held in the Queen's Park. That year the inspecting officer was to be Field-Marshal Lord Roberts, but, at the last moment, he had to call off.

Tommy had ordered two tickets for his parents and went to fetch them on the Friday evening. " Perhaps your parents won't want to come now that Lord Roberts is not to be there," suggested the captain.

" Oh," said the youngster, drawing himself up, " they are not coming to see Lord Roberts. They are coming to see *me!*"

QUEEN VICTORIA did not suffer fools gladly amongst older people, but had a soft heart for children. One summer at Balmoral she promised the child of a workman on the estate that she would bring her a doll from London on her return the following year.

It seemed to the girl too much to hope that the great lady with all her duties of State should remember. But, the following year, imagine the delight of the child when the first visit the Queen made on her return to Balmoral was to the cottage with the doll.

Part of the greatness of Queen Victoria was due in no small way to her concern for individuals, no matter how humble. Little wonder she was so well loved.

THE FRIENDSHIP BOOK

SUNDAY—JANUARY 18.

FOR we walk by faith, not by sight.

MONDAY—JANUARY 19.

NO use sighing, no use crying,
Just a waste of breath to say,
" If I'm lucky, p'raps tomorrow
Things will start to go my way."
Help a neighbour, do a kindness,
Gather sunny smiles today !

TUESDAY—JANUARY 20.

VISITORS to London make a point of seeing Cleopatra's Needle, the famous monument on the Thames Embankment. It is so old that it is said Moses might have read the inscription on its side.

It came from Egypt, the only thing discovered after the sand had obliterated cities and all traces of civilisation. When they dismantled it for removal to London they found in it relics of the age in which it had been built, children's toys and dolls, little mirrors that the ladies of the day used, bangles and jewellery.

When it was rebuilt in London last century they placed in it children's toys and playthings, mirrors of the times, a telephone directory and all the national newspapers of the day, photos of the most beautiful women in London, and a packet of ordinary razor blades. The intention was that if London ever crumbles to dust, these might survive as typical of our age.

Aren't we all building our own memorials day by day, doing things by which we will be remembered in the years to come?

CHANGE

Empty the towers, silent the walls,
No man at arms his challenge calls,
And where the baron once held sway
Picnicking children come to play.

DAVID HOPE

SAFE HAVEN

Houses snuggled among the trees,
  For yachts a sheltered mooring space.
They would be hard indeed to please
  Who scorned the charms of such a place.

DAVID HOPE

WEDNESDAY—JANUARY 21.

DONALD ROBERTSON, of Bruntsfield, Edinburgh, was awakened at exactly twenty-four minutes past three in the morning by his telephone ringing. With a start, he ran downstairs, lifted the phone, and was alarmed to hear his mother's voice.

Anxiously he asked her what was wrong. "Nothing," she replied. "Everything's all right." Mystified, he asked her why she'd phoned. "To wish you happy birthday," she said. Donald swallowed. "Mum," he sighed patiently, "surely it could have waited until morning."

His mother laughed. "Son," she said, "I was lying awake here thinking about you and I remembered that exactly forty years ago, to the very minute, *you* got *me* out of my bed . . . so I'm just getting my own back!"

THURSDAY—JANUARY 22.

CAMPBELL and McDonald had been such inseparable friends that those who knew them were surprised when McDonald broke off the friendship suddenly and they were no longer on speaking terms.

A mutual acquaintance inquired of McDonald what had caused the quarrel. "Oh," was the angry reply, "it is because of what happened at Glencoe and the treachery of the Campbells."

"But that was long ago," protested the astonished acquaintance. "Yes, but I only heard about it last week!" retorted McDonald.

It can be difficult at times to forget old scores or battles long ago and sometimes we inherit our prejudices (of race, colour, class or nationality) long after they have passed into history. To forgive and forget is to begin again.

FRIDAY—JANUARY 23.

A SLIM little book called "Tongue-Tied" must surely be one of the most outstanding works ever published, although you may never have heard of the author, Joey Deacon.

Joey was born a spastic, his arms and legs virtually useless, and he cannot feed himself, read or write. And only his friend Ernie can understand what he is saying. The book is really the work of four inseparable friends, all handicapped, who live in a hospital in Surrey. Joey told his life story to Ernie, who repeated the words to Michael, who wrote them down in laborious script ; and Tom, also unable to read or write, typed them letter by letter. It took a day to produce about five lines of typescript, and fourteen months altogether to finish the work.

Enough effort to last a lifetime, you might think —but Joey and his friends are at work on a second book already !

SATURDAY—JANUARY 24.

JOHN PAUL JONES was an officer in the U.S. Navy during the War of American Independence. When, during a naval battle, his boat was sinking and the British called upon him to surrender, he replied, " I have not yet begun to fight."

If some task seems a bit too much for me to cope with and I'm tempted to give up, I often think of John Paul Jones. *He* certainly didn't know when he was beaten — so *I* try a little harder myself.

SUNDAY—JANUARY 25.

BLESS them which persecute you : bless, and curse not.

MONDAY—JANUARY 26.

RUBY was a guide dog. One day she was walking along the edge of a harbour wall with her new mistress when the blind lady suddenly took a step to the right and fell into the water. Ruby, not forgetting her training, plunged in, too, and swam around keeping her mistress near to the harbour steps until help arrived. When the unfortunate lady had recovered, she explained that Ruby had correctly pulled her to the left, but she herself had been quite certain that her path lay to the right.

It is not easy to trust and have faith in those around us when we cannot see the way ahead ourselves ; but surely this story tells us that there are times when we must.

TUESDAY—JANUARY 27.

OLD Sandy Wood and his neighbour didn't see eye to eye. Their quarrel went from bad to worse until Sandy could think of little else. Eventually Sandy knew he was dying, and he called his children to his bedside and made a last request. It was a strange one. He wanted his grave to be outside the churchyard wall so that, on the day of the Last Trump, he would not have to waste time scrambling over the wall, but could be off down the hill to be first to put his side of the argument to his Maker.

You can see Sandy's gravestone today if you know where to look amongst the trees and bushes outside the wall of St Regulus Churchyard, near Cromarty in Ross-shire. Old Sandy died in 1690, and has been lying there since then, ready to put his case.

And I thought it was women who always had to have the last word!

THE FRIENDSHIP BOOK

WE'VE been away for two whole days —
Just Jim and me together;
The children are with Granny, and
Who cares about the weather ?
It's good to get away like this,
But coming home is perfect bliss !

THURSDAY—JANUARY 29.

QUITE frankly, I don't know what to think . . .
One cold winter's night I was on my way to visit a friend. The pavements were very icy and I'd trouble keeping my feet. A girl of about 10 or 11 came running round the corner. There was no one else about.

Suddenly she slipped and down she went on the pavement with a heavy thump. Worse, as she fell she caught her head a terrible crack against a stone wall. A moment later came the tears.

Naturally, I hurried forward to help her up. She was sobbing bitterly, and I knew she must have hurt herself. What could I do? If only the Lady of the House had been there she'd have known. But she wasn't. So I said to the child quietly, " Look— I'll take you home. Do you live far away?"

She didn't reply. Instead, she looked at me in alarm through her tears, shook my hand from her shoulder, and, still sobbing, ran off into the night. I stood there heart-sick and helpless.

Of course she was right, perfectly right. She was doing what no doubt her parents had taught her to do, what all sensible parents teach their children to do nowadays.

But what a sorry comment on this sad world that we must teach the innocent never to trust strangers.

FRIDAY—JANUARY 30.

A FRIEND of mine wishes he had told a lie the other day. Before you get too shocked I'd better explain. He spotted a bulky parcel from his wife's clothes shop and guessed from her air of suppressed excitement that something was up. When he was settled in his chair after dinner he wasn't at all surprised when she twirled into the room in a new coat, a bargain at the sales.

" Well," she said as she twirled, " how do you like it?" and then, as she stopped and saw his face, added, " Tell me the truth now."

Well, like the tactless man that he is, he told her.

Quietly the coat was laid away at the back of the wardrobe and a very disappointed wife joined her husband by the fire for a very quiet evening.

Just a little white lie would have done . . .

SATURDAY—JANUARY 31.

A S a young man, Mahatma Gandhi came from India to England to be educated and one of his exercises in English was writing out the Beatitudes from the Sermon on the Mount: " Blessed are the meek, for they shall inherit the earth," &c. Those words made a profound impression on him and later, when he was a lawyer and was sent to Africa, he decided to apply the philosophy of the Sermon on the Mount there. It worked, and soon Gandhi was earning £3000 a year.

He could have lived on there very comfortably, but he knew that back home in India many of his own people were starving. He gave away his money, took the vow of poverty, and consecrated his life to helping the poor and downtrodden.

" Blessed are the meek . . ."

FEBRUARY

BLESSED is he that considereth the poor : the Lord will deliver him in time of trouble.

IMAGINE a young man — a member of the Boys' Brigade at that — who didn't stand up for the National Anthem !

It happened in Cathcart South Church when the Netherlee B.B. band joined the Cathcart boys at an anniversary service.

The service was just starting when Alastair Jessiman, one of the Netherlee pipers, put his finger into one of the wee holes at the front of the pew where the Communion cloths are tied on. It stuck fast. And, try as he might, Alastair just couldn't get his finger out again !

The first hymn was announced—and a red-faced Alastair had to remain seated while all his comrades stood up. Other hymns followed, and still, to the mystification of the minister and congregation, Alastair sat in his place. Even when " God Save The Queen " was announced and the whole church rose as one, Alastair, highly mortified, had to stay where he was.

Valiantly, he bore the shame and the odd looks until, after the benediction, his plight was explained. Hastily, a bowl of soapy water was brought to the pew. Alastair's finger was liberally doused. Hey presto, out it popped—and a mighty relieved young man escaped to lead the waiting band from the kirk.

Thank goodness life has its smiles as well as its sorrows !

TUESDAY—FEBRUARY 3.

SOMETHING you said hurt someone dear,
And at the time you meant it —
An unkind, jealous, wounding thing,
But now, how you repent it!
Hard as it is, pray make amends —
One word — and you'll again be friends.

WEDNESDAY—FEBRUARY 4.

ONE thing the Queen and the Duke of Edinburgh have in common is a sense of humour. So they were greatly amused when, on one occasion, visiting the East End of London, the Duke said something to the Queen and a group of children nearby burst into laughter.

He had whispered to her, " Buck up, sweetheart, you're drooping." The group were children from an adjacent deaf and dumb school who were able to lip read.

In their silent world the deaf and dumb sometimes pick up comments not intended for them. A small compensation, perhaps, for the blessings of which they have been deprived.

THURSDAY—FEBRUARY 5.

JOHN SANDERS is organist and choirmaster of Gloucester Cathedral.

Just recently one of the small choirboys was asked whom he thought he and the others boys were singing for.

He screwed up his nose thoughtfully for a moment. " Jesus, I s'pose," he replied.

Then, seriously, he added, " But when we're just practising, we're singing for Mr Sanders."

There's a parable there, if you care to look for it.

FRIDAY—FEBRUARY 6.

WHAT a wonderful word " thank-you " is !
David Brown, of Leeds, writes to me :

" It is many years since I was a teacher in Sunday
School. I never thought I had achieved very much,
and when my work sometimes took me away from
home, I had to give up Sunday school teaching.

" Then, long afterwards, on a visit home, the
mother of one of my former Sunday school pupils
came up to me and said, ' I want to thank you for
all you did for Richard.'

" You've no idea," David Brown writes, " what
that meant to me." But I do. Take a bow, Richard's
mum.

SATURDAY—FEBRUARY 7.

BUSINESS took the Lady of the House and me
to a little town we knew years ago.

We remembered it as a very quiet place, set
among fields of buttercups, its red-roofed houses
gathered round a grey church tower and a big
pond where ducks swam, overlooked by a wee
shop with wooden benches outside the door.

But, oh, the change that met us. The buttercup
fields have given place to a housing estate. A block of
flats hides the church tower. Gone is the village pond,
and the ducks. The village store is now a garage.

In place of peace, there is bustle. Traffic roars
by and people now shop at a supermarket. We were
told there's also a bingo hall nearby. All of it,
I suppose, good in its way, but oh, how different !

The Lady of the House nodded sympathetically
as I sounded off about all the changes before us.
Then, with a wry smile, she added, " Who ever
heard of an improvement that made things better ?"

I'm sure you know what she meant.

SUNDAY—FEBRUARY 8.

WHOSOEVER will be chief among you, let him be your servant.

MONDAY—FEBRUARY 9.

IF you're away from home, you may find a sting in the tail of this story.

Mrs Ann Harris, of Auckland, New Zealand, left Scotland in 1956, with her husband and daughter. Her mother said she didn't mind her family leaving as long as they wrote regularly. And Mrs Harris always did. Two years ago she was home on a visit and was surprised when her mother took out a bag, which contained every letter Mrs Harris had written, obviously read over and over again. Mrs Harris had never realised her letters meant so much to her mother. But when she returned to New Zealand, she vowed to write two letters a week, and she did.

Well, Mrs Harris's mother died last year, the letters still among her most treasured possessions. In telling me about it, Mrs Harris asked, " Can you imagine how much harder the blow would have been to bear had I not given her a few minutes of my time every week?"

Does the question sting you? If it does, start writing now . . .

TUESDAY—FEBRUARY 10.

AN observation from my old friend Bob Brownlee, of Red Deer, Alberta. A letter sent by Bob says :

" The only money that goes as far as it used to is the penny that rolls under the bed."

How true in these days of inflation.

WEDNESDAY—FEBRUARY 11.

ONE of my friends was among a group of Polish women in a Russian labour camp who, just after the war, organised a knitting competition. They used stripped twigs as needles and scraps of wool unravelled from a jumper that someone had discarded as the weather became a little warmer. Everyone had contributed a few grains of sugar from their meagre ration of two spoonfuls a day towards the prize ; the winner was to receive *three* spoonfuls for the best garment.

My friend was the winner with a minute swim-suit, and she tells me that even now she never takes for granted being able to buy a pound of sugar in the shops. She still remembers so vividly how much three spoonfuls meant to her all those years ago.

THURSDAY—FEBRUARY 12.

THERE can be few better-known figures in Kirkintilloch than Willie McLeary.

From the end of the First World War until he retired, he was the man who collected the money from the gas-meters in the town. He also collected many a true story.

One was of five-year-old Hughie who'd just lost his first tooth; he put it under his pillow and found sixpence in its place in the morning. When his chum heard of the fairy who exchanged sixpences for teeth, he was vastly impressed.

Later that day, as they kicked a ball about the backyard, the boys knocked over a dustbin. When they cleared up the mess, among the rubbish they found an old set of false teeth.

" Look, Hughie," said his pal, wide-eyed. " Our fortune's made !"

FRIDAY—FEBRUARY 13.

MY old headmaster had a favourite saying.

I can see him yet, thumbs hooked in his dusty black gown, peering over his steel spectacles, and saying in the deep, slow voice we feared and respected, " Always remember, boy, that good enough is *not* good enough."

Well, I have always remembered it. And I recalled it again when I had a letter from an elderly lady who was a NAAFI girl during the war.

Phyllis used to drive the mobile canteen round the various workshops and hangars on an airfield of Fighter Command. The Hurricanes and Spitfires based there had seen a lot of service. Repairs had to be quick—but they also had to be thorough.

And Phyllis tells me she'll never forget a huge notice-board at the entrance to the repair hangar. In big, black letters, it proclaimed :

" That'll do WON'T do "

Only four words from the 1940's. But have you heard a better motto for the 1970's?

SATURDAY—FEBRUARY 14.

*N*EVER is it easy
    Plodding on and on
When the weather's cruel,
    When your hopes are gone.
But to those with courage
    (*If they smile and sing*),
Sooner than expected
    Winter turns to spring!

SUNDAY—FEBRUARY 15.

THE Son of man is come to save that which was lost

MONDAY—FEBRUARY 16.

EVERY driver in the icy North comes to know the pullers and the slackers in his sleigh dog team.

I dare say, it is the same with people. I found it all summed up under the title, " Which Bone?"

Wishbones.—Those who want somebody else to do the work.

Jawbones.—Those who talk a lot and do little else.

Knucklebones.—Those who knuckle under and give in too easily.

Backbones.—Those who roll up their sleeves and get on with the work.

Or, to put it another way, the world is full of willing people: those who are willing to work—and those who are willing to let them !

TUESDAY—FEBRUARY 17.

IT'S easy singing merrily
When brightly shines the sun;
It's easy smiling cheerily
When life is mostly fun.
But hard it is to sing when sad,
When much concerned, to smile.
So very hard, as you well know —
But ALWAYS it's worth while!

WEDNESDAY—FEBRUARY 18.

THE Japanese saint, Toyohiko Kagawa, once made this pungent observation :

" I read in a book that a man called Christ went about *doing good*. It is very disconcerting to me that I am so easily satisfied with just going about."

To realise where one is failing others, is a first step, and an invaluable one.

THURSDAY—FEBRUARY 19.

A SMALL incident in Germany in 1916 had far-reaching consequences.

Dr Klaus Rimmer was idly looking out of the window at his beautiful garden, while speaking on the telephone, when, to his consternation, he saw one of his patients, a blind soldier, making his way uncertainly over the lawn.

The soldier, Captain Fleitel, was going straight towards a tree, but before he could come to harm, Dr Rimmer's Alsatian, Frieda, appeared silently and gently stopped the soldier in his tracks by standing broadside in his path.

Dr Rimmer watched as the dog led the soldier round the tree and in between the flower beds.

From this apparently trivial happening, the idea of Guide Dogs for the Blind was born.

FRIDAY—FEBRUARY 20.

MRS GRANT and her husband, when I dropped in to see them, had been decorating the living-room. Tom had decided to change things round a bit.

" That mirror, now," he said. " Couldn't we put it on the opposite wall ? Then you could put that picture where the mirror is."

" No," said Mrs Grant.

" Why ? What difference does it make ?"

" Well, you see, it tells me when spring is here. Just for two or three days, early on, the sun strikes the mirror, and the bevel makes a sort of rainbow on the wall. If I leave the kitchen door open, the colours shine through on to the washing-machine, and then I know the daffodils will soon be out . . ."

Tom, you'll be glad to know, gave in. You can't beat a woman's logic.

SATURDAY—FEBRUARY 21.

MY innocent remark to a minister the other day set him thinking when, at a wedding reception, I said to him, " You must be tired of weddings. To you one must be just the same as another."

He agreed and then his eyes twinkled. " Except once I followed the wrong bride to the reception at a hotel and was in the middle of proposing the toast to her before I realised my mistake !"

That started a string of stories. The most moving was when a British soldier was marrying a German girl. She knew English and could follow the service, but her parents and sister had come from Germany to see her married and understood not a word.

" Then," continued the minister, " when we came to repeating the Lord's Prayer they broke their silence and joined in."

That wonderful prayer united them as one.

SUNDAY—FEBRUARY 22.

IN lowliness of mind let each esteem other better than themselves.

MONDAY—FEBRUARY 23.

I MAY not strive to reach the heights,
My place is lowly and obscure;
But if at night I can recall
One helpful deed, however small;
If some bright word I may have said
A soul has cheered and comforted;
If I have tried at least to share
The burdens that my neighbours bear,
Then I may count my day well spent,
And sleep with calm and sweet content.

THE FRIENDSHIP BOOK

TUESDAY—FEBRUARY 24.

READING an old book the other day, I came upon a little story about the novelist Sir Walter Scott. In his own inimitable style of writing, he put into a nutshell how many of us feel first thing in the morning. He said that he found that beginning the day's work was " as distasteful as plunging into cold water. We shiver on the brink," he said, " but once in, are full of vigour and energy."

Maybe we ought to follow the advice of the philosopher who said, " Don't wonder *when* to do a thing, just do it *now* !"

WEDNESDAY—FEBRUARY 25.

AGASSIZ, the Italian scholar, in his lifetime impressed everybody with his goodness, tolerance and understanding.

One day he disclosed his secret. As a little boy he had been taken by his mother to a hill facing another over a valley and told if he spoke the little boy on the other side would answer.

" Who are you ?" shouted Agassiz and back came the answer, " Who are you ?"

" I don't like you," he called and there came the answer, " I don't like you." " I think you are a nasty boy," and in return, " I think you are a nasty boy."

" Try something nice," suggested his mother. Agassiz shouted, " Will you come and play with me ?" and back came, " come and play with me ?" And finally, " I think you are a nice boy " in mutual exchange.

Of course, Agassiz soon found out that the voice across the valley was only an echo, but he realised from this that one's friends are an echo of ourselves. If they have faults—don't we perhaps share them?

THE FRIENDSHIP BOOK

THE warm and sunny days, no doubt,
Are quite a long way off;
There may be snow, high winds may blow —
I've still a hacking cough!
But dawn comes sooner. Some birds sing.
I'll keep on keeping on till spring!

FRIDAY—FEBRUARY 27.

MRS MACKAY was in tears because someone offered her a £5 note.

She lives in a city tenement, a widow and a pensioner. When her neighbour's husband died, his wife took it badly. She refused to eat, and wouldn't go out. Her son, who lives in town, didn't seem able to help.

Mrs Mackay popped in to see what she could do. She took in small, but tempting meals. She went out for errands. She came in at night—the worst time of all—just to be there. For five weeks, Mrs Mackay did what she felt a good neighbour should do, and at the end of it the widow across the landing had picked up the threads of life again.

Her son was so thankful, and he wanted to show his gratitude to Mrs Mackay for all she'd done. So just as he was leaving one night, he put a £5 note on his mother's sideboard, and told her to pass it on to Mrs Mackay. He thought she'd be glad of the extra.

Well, she wasn't. What she had done for her neighbour came from the goodness of her heart. By offering her money, a well-meaning, but thoughtless young man seemed to be putting a price on all she'd done and had tarnished the glow.

Kindness, like honesty, is its own reward— and that £5 left on the sideboard just spoiled things.

AT PEACE

It is a timeless pleasure they enjoy,
  Gliding past scenes unchanged for centuries.
A hundred years from now will girl and boy
  Find peace like them beneath the willow trees?

DAVID HOPE

WELCOME

Sometimes early, sometimes late,
Sometimes long past the date;
Sometimes chilly, sometimes mild,
Often still—more often wild!

Sometimes slow and sometimes fast,
(Is she really here at last?)
Sometimes bright and sometimes grey,
But Springtime's welcome anyway.

DAVID HOPE.

JOY OF LIFE

When the wind blows over the hills
And blue is the sky,
We like to go out on the moor,
My mistress and I.
And the world's full of fun
As I run — and I run — and I run!

DAVID HOPE

THE FRIENDSHIP BOOK

PICTURE a soldier sitting with his comrades in their billet in North Africa during the war.

The radio is playing. Suddenly a quiet, friendly voice starts speaking—and, to his surprise, one of the soldiers hears his name mentioned, and those of his father, mother and brother. Then the music starts again—" I'll Walk Beside You."

The voice was that of Sandy Macpherson, the BBC theatre organist for 25 years. The tune was requested by the soldier's father for his two boys —one in Africa and one in the Navy—and his wife, seriously ill, but listening, too. Somehow, that old song brought them all together and, a few weeks later, Sandy had a letter to say that sick mother had taken a turn for the better.

That was only one of the countless rewards Sandy's programme brought him. At its peak during the war, 3000 letters a week reached him— mothers asking for tunes for their sons; soldiers requesting songs for wives, sweethearts and mothers; and many more.

Over and over again, Sandy would hear how an old, familiar tune, sent with love, had helped to mend a marriage almost on the rocks, to heal a broken heart and to comfort one in sorrow. He treasured them all.

Last year this quiet and gentle Canadian, whose mother came from Forfar and whose father came from Badenoch, died at 78. I'm sure this story helps to show why, in many homes, he is recalled with true affection.

FOR by grace are ye saved through faith : and that not of yourselves : it is the gift of God.

MARCH

MONDAY—MARCH 1.

DO we always appreciate the lessons our parents teach us?

The thought came to me after speaking to a friend I hadn't seen for some time.

She was one of a family of six. She recalled how proud her mother was when they moved from a tenement to a house with a small garden. It had been neglected for years, but mother had the family out digging, weeding, working it into shape. Then they built a rockery, planted bulbs and sowed flowers. Often, of course, the children rebelled. Always mother said, " No, do your stint. I'll explain it all on my birthday."

Then on that sunny morning, she took them outside and said, " I want you all to remember your lives, your work and your marriages will often be the same as this garden. Sometimes you must buckle down to what you don't want to do. But if you do it with care and love, the day will come when you can do as we're doing now, stand back, see the flowers bloom and realise what you've gained."

Her daughter never forgot that morning in the garden and how much she learned from it.

TUESDAY—MARCH 2.

*Y*OU'RE *man and wife? Because life's tough*
    You may be cross or sad —
Or even snap a little bit
    When things get very bad.
The roof may fall in, but no doubt
The two of you will not fall out!

WEDNESDAY—MARCH 3.

A FEW miles from my home is a wood which is loved for its daffodils in the spring. Ever since I was small, I have gone along to see the daffodils at least once a year.

Last year, I missed them. I intended to go, but you know how it is. I had lots of other things to do, and when I did manage to visit the wood, they were gone.

I was so vexed with myself. I felt as if I had let God down—for, after all, He'd made that yellow loveliness for me, and I'd never even bothered to go and see it, or thank Him for it.

I'm sure you know just how I felt.

THURSDAY—MARCH 4.

IF it makes you smile, that's good. But if it makes you think, so much the better.

I refer to a notice in big red letters I saw posted up outside a city church.

" Try this church for a month," it proclaimed. " If you don't like what you hear, your sins will be cheerfully refunded."

Who could resist an offer like that ?

FRIDAY—MARCH 5.

HERE is an old Arab saying that is worth thinking about :

" A real friend is a person to whom you can bring the contents of your heart, and empty them out—chaff and grain together. The gentlest hands will then take it and sift it, keeping hold of what is worth holding and gently blowing the rest away."

How many of us can be sure that our friends could say that of us ?

THE FRIENDSHIP BOOK

YOU'VE to be up early to hear the dawn chorus.
But I know of a man who listened to the birds singing their dawn chorus at teatime.

Rab Lindsay, a young joiner from Dunlop, Ayrshire, spent no fewer than six spells in hospital in three years. He knew how weary the hours there could be, so, when he went back into Kilmarnock Hospital again, he went prepared.

He took a small tape-recorder with the voices of his wife and his friends. And when little else could comfort him, his wife's words carried him through the bad patch.

Then early one morning, while most of the other patients were still asleep, Rab called the nurse to his bed. All he asked was that she might open the window wide, for Rab wanted to tape the dawn chorus, so he could listen over and over again to its simple beauty.

That is why, as I say, he heard it at teatime, and why one of the last things he heard before he died was the song of the birds welcoming a new and glorious dawn . . .

SET your affection on things above, not on things on the earth.

A THOUSAND pities should March pass
Without you seeing fresh green grass,
Or (far too busy all day long)
You never hear the skylark's song,
Or know some magic moment spent
Amid a garden's springtime scent.

THE FRIENDSHIP BOOK

TUESDAY—MARCH 9.

WOULD you pay £300 for a fireside rug that isn't perfect?

It seems the men who weave Persian carpets are among the world's most skilful craftsmen. Every carpet is a work of art—to almost every eye, as to mine, each is perfect. But the Persian carpet weavers believe that only God—or, as they say, Allah—can create true perfection. So somewhere in every carpet, they weave a deliberate mistake, a hidden flaw. Only an expert can detect it—indeed, it is one of the ways they can tell the carpet is a genuine Persian one—but the weaver himself knows it is there, and that is the point.

It helps to keep him humble. It guards him from the sin of pride. And though he knows he will never achieve perfection, it does not keep him from striving for it.

Perhaps it does seem strange to us, yet if we only opened our eyes to the hidden flaws in ourselves . . .

WEDNESDAY—MARCH 10.

DAVID'S new bike is his pride and joy. He got it for his fifth birthday—a real two-wheeler with a carrier at the back and a bright, shining bell that resounded up and down our quiet street all week.

But yesterday, something else resounded—David bawling his head off! The Lady of the House dashed out and, sure enough, he'd come a cropper.

"What happened, dear?" she said, kneeling to comfort him. David turned a tear-stained face to her.

"I fell off," he sobbed. "My front wheel tripped!"

STOP! Take time to read this :—
Take time to think;
It is the source of power.
Take time to play;
It is the secret of perpetual youth.
Take time to read;
It is the fountain of wisdom.
Take time to pray;
It is the greatest power on earth.
Take time to love and be loved;
It is a God-given privilege.
Take time to laugh;
It is the music of the soul.
Take time to give;
It is too short a day to be selfish.
Take time to work;
It is the price of success.

FRIDAY—MARCH 12.

ROY SUTHERLAND, of Bruntsfield, Edinburgh, has a friend who is a traveller.

The other day, the traveller was in a village store when a small boy came in with two empty lemonade bottles. He planked them down on the counter, waited while the grocer counted out six pennies, and immediately asked for a large ice-cream cone.

" He's my best customer," smiled the grocer, winking at the traveller. " He brings me lemonade bottles most days and buys a cone." Then he paused. " Incidentally, son," he said, " where on earth do you collect so many empty bottles ?"

" Oh," replied the wee lad innocently, accepting his cone, " there's a big heap of them in your back yard."

SATURDAY—MARCH 13.

A THOUGHTLESS word, a chance remark—
  You didn't really mean it;
But someone's hurt. It's left a wound—
  You couldn't have foreseen it.
Today, I beg you, make amends—
Tomorrow, you'll once more be friends.

SUNDAY—MARCH 14.

IN God I have put my trust : I will not be afraid what man can do unto me.

MONDAY—MARCH 15.

DID you know a woman's knitting may show what kind of a person she is ?

Old Mrs Howie lives with her married daughter in Dundee. She received a present of a bed cape knitted by a friend of the Lady of the House, who sent it to the old lady.

A few days later a letter came from Mrs Howie, thanking us and wondering how we knew about her. " I don't suppose I'll ever know who knitted the cape," she added, " but it's beautiful, and I know she's a happy person, whoever she is.

" You see," she said, " I've noticed over the years that when somebody who's sad or worried or angry knits something, the stitches are always tight—because, even if they don't realise it, they pull a little bit too hard on the wool, or hold their needles too tight." Then she went on, " But happy, contented, friendly people knit looser, slacker stitches, so everything seems softer and warmer somehow, like this cape."

That pink cape means all the more to Mrs Howie because it was knitted with love.

TUESDAY—MARCH 16.

THE other day the Lady of the House was looking at curtain material.

The young shop assistant cut off the required length of material, wrapped it up, and with a bright smile she told her customer, " My great-grandad's ninety today. I've just been speaking to him on the phone and he's as bright as ever. I'll be over to see him as soon as I finish here. I just can't wait to see him."

Ninety, and still going strong That's something to be proud of and thankful for. But to be ninety and still loved . . . ah, that's something quite wonderful.

WEDNESDAY—MARCH 17.

GOT some unpleasant task to do?
  Don't do it by and by.
Begin it now, don't put it off —
  And here's the reason why.
You won't enjoy it? Then what fun
When you can say that task is done.

THURSDAY—MARCH 18.

MAYBE you've heard the story of the farmer who was getting slightly deaf.

He didn't want to spend money on a hearing aid so he tucked one end of a piece of string into his shirt collar and curled the other end behind his ear. It worked because everyone, on seeing the string, spoke louder.

An old friend who has begun to wear a hearing aid complained that people are now shouting at her. She continued, " If only they had spoken up before I wouldn't be wearing this contraption now."

LUCKY PEOPLE

Among the trees thatch looks exactly right,
As though the houses naturally grew,
For passing city folk a charming sight,
Home for the happy few.

DAVID HOPE

LONDON TULIPS

I love the town in May-time
When cold winter's taken wing.
But I'll let you into a secret—
I love everywhere in spring.

DAVID HOPE

FRIDAY—MARCH 19.

SOME would have you believe the age of chivalry is dead.

Not according to this incident which, I'm told, took place in an Aberdeen church while the collection was being taken up. It seems an elderly woman had forgotten to bring her offering. She was fumbling through her handbag, getting more and more flustered as the plate drew nearer.

But her plight did not go unnoticed. A wee lad of five was sitting in the same pew with his mother and father, and saw her consternation. Quietly, he sidled along the cushion towards her, and slipped her a 2p piece.

"Here, missus," he whispered gallantly. "You take my penny, and I'll hide under the seat."

SATURDAY—MARCH 20.

WHEN Scots divinity students have completed their college course, they have to serve for a year as probationer assistants under the guidance of a minister. And, it may be said, under the watchful eye of the congregation who are sympathetic with mistakes.

The first appearance in a pulpit may be trying to a nervous youth. One had prepared to the last word. But as he finished the scripture reading it was obvious he was in difficulty how to end. After a pause the congregation were amused to hear him say, " . . . er . . . we propose a vote of thanks for this reading."

It must be a proud moment for them, but it was rather shattering for one who, as he entered the pulpit, overheard a small boy say in a voice that could be heard all over the church, " Mum, it won't be much of a sermon today. It's just the *apprentice*."

SUNDAY—MARCH 21.

BE ye kind one to another, tenderhearted, forgiving one another, even as God for Christ's sake hath forgiven you.

MONDAY—MARCH 22.

ON the way home from church one Sunday, I walked with a friend.

" You know, Francis," he said, " I often wonder if many of us really know what love is. I think I first saw it in action in the kitchen at home when I happened to notice that while my mother was paring potatoes at the sink she was resting her right knee on a stool . . . just to give her aching leg a bit of support and comfort.

" I never heard my mother complain though I often saw her wince. She kept on and on till one day she collapsed, and died soon after. Love gave her strength to serve and bless her loved ones. It never even occurred to her to ease up—she loved us all so much that it was easier keeping on in anguish than sitting back."

If God's love is greater than a mother's care, how very, very great it must be.

TUESDAY—MARCH 23.

AT a wedding I attended, the following advice was quoted by the minister to a newly-married pair :

" I want to give you this message, my children—don't try to be happy. Happiness is a shy nymph, and if you chase her you will never catch her. Just go quietly along, doing your duty, and she will come to you."

And you know, it works !

WEDNESDAY—MARCH 24.

MAUREEN HARRISON, of Leicester, sends me this story with a smile.

A Sunday school teacher had been telling her class about the armour of God—the breastplate of righteousness, the shield of faith, the helmet of salvation, and so on.

" But there's something else we must carry," she added, referring, of course, to the sword of the spirit. " It's very sharp, and it cuts — d'you remember what it is ?"

For a moment there was silence. Then one wee girl's face brightened, and up went her hand.

" Please, Miss," she cried triumphantly, " it's the axe of the apostles."

THURSDAY—MARCH 25.

RECENTLY a Glasgow lady wrote to ask me about something that has been puzzling her.

It is this. There are lots of people who never go to church, yet seem just as good as those who do. If so, does this mean we could get on just as well without the Church ?

I passed on the question to an old lady whose wisdom helps me sometimes when I am stuck.

She smiled and said, " When were you in a grocer's shop last ? Months ago ? Or when were you last down a mine digging coal ? Never ?"

I thought she was wandering a bit, but she continued, " And yet you've always had breakfast, dinner and tea laid on the table, and you've always had a bit of fire and light at nights. Shut the grocers' shops and the coal mines, and you'll soon know the difference."

I am sure she has something there. Shut the churches, and we'd soon know the difference.

THE FRIENDSHIP BOOK

THE old lady was crying when the minister visited her. She was blind, finally, after a gradual failing of her sight and now she felt she was at the end of her tether. " I can't see," she said " I can't find my way about, and I don't know what to do."

" Right," said the minister. " First of all, get down on your knees. Now, feel with your hands where you are. Now go round the room, feeling all the time." When she had learned the whereabouts of all the chairs, and got to know the room, not as she had known it as a sighted person, but as a blind person who relies on touch, he took her round again with his stick in her hand. " Keep the stick," he said to her when he left. " And remember, whenever you need me, don't be afraid to let me know."

" I never looked back after that," said the old lady to me. " And mind you, there was a message in it, when I got to thinking. The first thing he told me was to get down on my knees . . . "

SATURDAY—MARCH 27.

I'VE heard some prima donnas
In oratorios;
I've heard the singing film stars
Whom everybody knows;
But they, with all their top C's,
Their tantrums and their art,
Have never quite enchanted,
Or run off with my heart,
As my own darling Mary,
Who sings a simple song,
To brighten up the morning
And help the chores along!

THE FRIENDSHIP BOOK

SUNDAY—MARCH 28.

BUT many that are first shall be last; and the last shall be first.

MONDAY—MARCH 29.

ONE evening, an elderly couple strolled in the gloaming round a little bay on the Western Isle of Colonsay.

There, among the flotsam, they came on a great baulk of timber, thick with barnacles, ugly and clumsy as it floundered among the breakers.

Most of us, I suppose, would have passed it by, but, by chance, woodwork was the man's lifelong hobby. So, taking a knife, he cut a sliver from the great log. " Nigerian mahogany! " he exclaimed to his wife, as though he'd found treasure, as indeed to him he had, for it is one of the noblest of timbers.

At that moment, it came to the man that here surely was a God-given chance to repay Colonsay for the many joyful holidays he and his wife had spent there. And so he began the long task of acquiring the log from the Receiver of Wrecks, of shipping it to Leith, of getting a sawmill to cut it into planks, and, finally, in his own home in Edinburgh, of lovingly fashioning the wood into his gift to Colonsay : a magnificent Communion chair.

The woodworker, I may say, was Mr A. E. Robertson, himself a minister who now, alas, had passed on. But his chair still stands in the little island kirk, admired by all, though most do not know the secret of its transformation.

If they did, I'm sure they would agree that the great message of the chair is that there is beauty to be found wherever we look, if only we look.

THE FRIENDSHIP BOOK

AT 25, Christopher Wren was appointed Professor of Astronomy at Gresham College, London.

At the age of 77 Sir Christopher saw the last stone laid on the tip of the lantern of St Paul's Cathedral, and the great ball and cross placed in position, crowning the glory of the dome.

The astronomer had become the architect, the architect who looked heavenwards with his designs. There were domes, there were towers, and an abundance of wonderful steeples among the 52 churches Wren designed. The habit of looking upward towards the heavens, so firmly established when he was young, was never forgotten.

Who knows what we may achieve if we, too, keep looking upwards.

I HEARD recently of a girl of five who was attempting to get into a new jumper.

Somehow in her struggles she got her head into a sleeve, and from the woollen prison in which she found herself she was heard to exclaim, " Some people can be very lonely in a jumper."

People can be lonely in unexpected places. I myself was never so lonely as when I was odd man out at a party. I was only 18. Everybody knew everybody else, but nobody knew me. In the end I slipped quietly away—a silly thing to do, I admit, but I felt less lonely going home in the dark than I had felt at that lively party.

And few folk are more lonely than those who have a deep worry at the back of their mind, a fear of tomorrow, or a sorrow they can't share.

Maybe someone you know is going through some ordeal at this time . . .

APRIL

THURSDAY—APRIL 1.

I'M sure the Rev. Alex. Russell, of Alexandria, Dunbartonshire, won't mind me passing on this story from one of his congregation.

It seems that the year when April 1 was a Sunday, Mr Russell announced from the pulpit that the text for the boys' and girls' lesson was to be Hezekiah, Chapter 1, verse 3.

There were puzzled looks as the congregation searched for the verse in their Bibles. Pages were flipped back and forward. Surreptitious glances were slipped to see if neighbours in the pew had found the place. Then Mr Russell called out, "You've all been April Fooled! There is no book of Hezekiah."

For a moment there was silence, then a wave of laughter spread throughout the church. And why not? You don't need to be dull to be serious, do you?

FRIDAY—APRIL 2.

ODD how you can sometimes pick up pearls for nothing.

Only the other day I was looking for a book in the library and quite by chance picked up a copy of " Love at Paddington," by William Pett Ridge, who died over forty years ago.

Thumbing a page or two of his book, I found this simple bit of philosophy :

" If you want to view trouble you could take opera-glasses—but you should be careful to hold them the wrong way round."

Bear it in mind when things go wrong.

SATURDAY—APRIL 3.

MISS ALISON, now three years old,
  May call on Mrs Gray,
And chat to her, or sing a song
  In her own charming way.
Oh, what a thrill at ninety-four
To see an angel at your door!

SUNDAY—APRIL 4.

IN the beginning God created the heaven and the earth.

MONDAY—APRIL 5.

YOU may think there is not much in this story—but here it is, anyway.

A friend of mine in London, leaving Euston Station saw a slight commotion on the busy road outside.

A pigeon had been struck a glancing blow by a passing bus, injuring its wing. Dazed, it fluttered from the pavement into the road.

It looked like curtains for the pigeon. But, no! A taxi screeched to a stop only inches away from it. The driver jumped out, waved down the rest of the traffic—and four lanes of lorries, buses and cars came to a halt as he chased the pigeon over the road, and finally caught it.

Cradling it tenderly in his hands, he carried it back to his taxi. " Well done," said my friend. The cabby grinned, half-apologetically. " Couldn't leave the poor thing there, could I?" he said. " I'll soon have that wing mended." And off he drove.

I dare say there are more important things in London to write about. But I'm glad I heard this story and I gladly pass it on.

THE FRIENDSHIP BOOK

WHEN I was a schoolboy aged about nine, my home was about two miles from school. Cycling there on a bright, sunny morning was easy as pie, because the road was downhill almost all the way. Coming home, however, was another story—pedalling uphill was a tiring job.

One winter's day I cycled home after darkness had fallen. Street lamps were very few and far between. I pedalled on and on till suddenly I stopped short. A street lamp at a corner lit up the outside of *my* house . . . I had arrived sooner than expected, less tired than before, and then, very puzzled, I realised what had happened. I'd been pedalling into the darkness, seeing only a few square yards of what looked like a flat road picked out by the short, weak beam of my cycle lamp.

Even at the early age of nine I realised that if you don't keep looking up your hill, climbing it is easier.

I DON'T know who Mary is, but I have heard about her. Jeannie was her best school pal, and they were inseparable. But, as children will, they quarrelled, and for days did not speak to one another.

Then Jeannie contracted measles. She was astonished when Mary not only visited her, but, taking off her shoes, climbed into bed beside her.

" But, Mary," exclaimed Jeannie horrified, " you'll catch measles, too ! " " I don't care," replied Mary, " I just wanted to show you how much I love you."

Could they keep up a quarrel after that? The first step in reconciliation may so often be to show how far love is willing to go.

THURSDAY—APRIL 8.

BLAME everybody but yourself,
  Be scowling, sour and sad;
Let bitterness dog every step,
  Look only for the bad.
That's how, from hope, to dull each gleam,
And dig a grave for every dream.

FRIDAY—APRIL 9.

SOME time ago a very sick friend was told by her doctor that she might live only a matter of months. She did not weep or cry out against God. Her only regret was the thought of leaving her husband and little daughter.

Carefully she began to plan for each precious day. The meals were prepared and the table set as if for some festive occasion. She listened for her husband's returning footsteps each evening and ran to meet him.

Together they would prepare their little girl for bed, taking turns at reading her favourite stories. They never hurried over the task, for their time together was growing short. Each precious minute must be enjoyed.

Then one day when she went to the hospital she was told there had been a mistake. She was not going to die.

Hurrying home in the sunshine, she was too stunned at first to take in just what this wonderful news meant. She was not going to die. Her joy was so intense she felt as if a shower of stars exploded all round her. " I am not going to die," she kept repeating, " it's all a mistake."

Later she told me how the mistake had taught her to treasure every single moment of every day.

SATURDAY—APRIL 10.

VISITORS to Southend in the Mull of Kintyre are always told that from the Mull they can see five kingdoms. The Kingdom of Scotland, of course; the Kingdom of Ireland; the Kingdom of England in the shape of the Cumberland hills; and the Kingdom of Man, a distant smudge in the Irish Sea.

"But you said ' five kingdoms.' "

"Sure. There's also the Kingdom of Heaven !"

SUNDAY—APRIL 11.

LET all those that put their trust in thee rejoice.

MONDAY—APRIL 12.

WHEN we are sad and all alone
    And tears fall thick and fast
We bow our heads and fate bemoan,
    We think our grief will last.
But if we chance to raise our eyes
    And look towards the light
We find our help comes from the skies
    And hope grows clear and bright.
Someone up there knows all our fears,
    He watches from above,
Our Father up in Heav'n Who sees
    Will comfort us with love.
If humbly from our hearts we pray
    With pure and simple tongue,
Despair and sadness fade away,
    We do not wait for long
For smiles to take the place of tears,
    For joy instead of pain;
When faith has banished all our fears
    We tread the path again.

TUESDAY—APRIL 13.

MRS NASH hates spring cleaning. She used to say there was so much to do that she didn't know where to start—so she couldn't bring herself to start at all.

Now she has what she calls her " system." She lists every job that has to be done—and a long, long list it is. Then she begins—anywhere; and as every job is done she scores it off.

Quite often she gets bogged down and feels she's getting nowhere, but a glance at her list shows her she's done quite a lot; and one day she finds that she's left with a sheet of paper completely covered with black marks!

" I never thought I could do it," she said to me, " but somehow, when you do one job at a time you get through the lot without noticing."

It's like that with life. We couldn't possibly take it all on at once. A day at a time gets you there.

WEDNESDAY—APRIL 14.

A NEIGHBOUR'S boy of six is anything but an angel.

He's a typical youngster, mad about football, cars, cowboys and the like.

When he heard that one of his school chums (a boy he'd had a fight with only a few days before) was at home with a broken leg, he asked if he could visit him and take him something.

His mother made a few suggestions, but the boy suddenly ran off to his room and came back with the model car he prized most. "I'll be sorry to give Peter this," he said, " but I've got to! It's no use giving a pal something you don't want, is it, Mum?"

Mum agreed—but I believe Dad is arranging, after a suitable time, to replace the precious car!

THURSDAY—APRIL 15.

THE lives that boast no need of faith have no foundation stone. Their minds can never be at ease no matter where they roam. Without a knowledge sure and true that God is everywhere, a life—in time of sorrow—can be plunged into despair.

There must be faith to bring the joy that we seek every day. The quiet understanding that brings peace at work or play. No one can build on shifting sand and hope then to survive. There must be deep foundations to keep your dream alive.

FRIDAY—APRIL 16.

I'D a letter the other day from Mrs Ferguson, of Arbroath, telling me about her friend, Katie Rooney, of Coatbridge.

Before she died, Katie was crippled by arthritis for almost 12 years, being cared for with love and gentleness by her husband, Joe. He was a gem, says Mrs Ferguson, and such a comfort.

That word " comfort " caught my eye. I'd been looking at a book which came to me years ago from an old uncle. Dry stuff, most of it, but then I came across the word " comfort." I'd always taken it to mean, simply, " console."

But Uncle John's book went further. It told me that it is made up of two words, the first of which means " with," and the second " strength." Originally, the word " comforter " meant " one who stands alongside to strengthen." To me, that's a far, far better description of what Mrs Ferguson meant when she was speaking of Joe Rooney. For 12 years he was a comfort to Katie—he stood alongside her and strengthened her.

So whenever I use that word I will remember that comfort gives not only consolation but courage.

SATURDAY—APRIL 17.

YOU have all heard the story of Greyfriars Bobby, I know, but do you know about Bluey?

Bluey was an Australian dog, who was the life-long companion of a swagman—a tramp, in Australia. Now one day Bluey's master was walking along the road accompanied by his dog when along came a car and knocked down the swagman. In due course the ambulance arrived and off went the injured man to hospital. Bluey, wondering what was going on, followed the ambulance all the way to the hospital, but, of course, wasn't allowed in.

He didn't know that his master had died, and so he continued his vigil for twelve years, being fed and looked after by many of the friends he made while he waited patiently for his master to return.

When he died, all those who had befriended him, and many people who had only heard of his fidelity, contributed to a fund, and to this day, in a hospital in Australia, there is a bed with a plaque above it reading " In memory of Bluey, a faithful friend."

SUNDAY—APRIL 18.

INASMUCH as ye have done it unto one of the least of these my brethren, ye have done it unto me.

MONDAY—APRIL 19.

CHRIST has no hands but our hands to do His work today;
He has no feet but our feet to lead men in the way;
He has no tongue but our tongues to tell men how He died;
He has no help but our help to bring them to His side.

THE FRIENDSHIP BOOK

THE other evening the Lady of the House sat down at the piano.

In front of her was a copy of a new hymn, " By the Rutted Roads we Follow." It is a hymn for spring-time, speaking of ploughing and planting, and of the patience and care that are needed before a harvest is reaped. In a sense, it is a parable about the secret of living.

But what intrigued us most was the name of the author. It is familiar to us, and I'm sure, to you—John Arlott. Could this be the same man to whom we listened on the radio as he gave his cricket commentaries?

Well, he is, indeed, the writer of that fine new hymn. And I also learned that John Arlott's own road has brought him many of life's bitter experiences. For four years he worked in a mental hospital. For 11 years, and right through the war, he was a policeman in Southampton, and witnessed much of the tragedy and devastation of those terrible times. His eldest son, only 20, was killed in a car crash.

Now, in his hymn, he is sharing with us the faith that carried him through, a prayer for every new beginning on life's road.

AN old friend, herself a bit hard of hearing, was telling the Lady of the House about a man who bought a new hearing aid.

It was very expensive, but he told his wife it was well worth the money, as he could now hear perfectly with it.

" Good," said his wife. " What kind is it?"

Replied the man, " Just after half-past five !"

THURSDAY—APRIL 22.

TRAVELLING through Gloucestershire, we came to Tewkesbury, where I was reminded of Mrs Craik, the writer of " John Halifax, Gentleman." She used the town of Tewkesbury as the background for her tale of the poor boy, left an orphan, dependent on his own efforts from the age of eleven. Movingly, she told of his willingness to do any kind of work that was honest, even if it was distasteful, of his high principles, his integrity and courage that eventually led him to happiness and prosperity.

Happiness and prosperity came to her much more rapidly. In 1864, within eight years of the publication of " John Halifax, Gentleman," she was given a Civil List pension of eighty pounds a year.

She lived as she wrote; and the compassionate imagination that enabled her to enter into the troubles of John Halifax prompted her to set this money aside for authors less fortunate than she was.

This, too, is worth remembering.

FRIDAY—APRIL 23.

IT'S funny the things that give us pleasure. Not only presents or good deeds done, but simply the unexpected visitor, or an old scrap of paper with a poem to cheer us along, like this one—
If you put a little loving into all the work you do,
A little bit of gladness, a little bit of you,
A little bit of sweetness, a little bit of song,
Not a day will seem so toilsome, not a day
    will seem so long.
Although the author is unknown, and it was written many years ago, the message still rings true, doesn't it ?

OLD FRIENDS

Companions in the truest sense,
They make a perfect team,
Founded on mutual confidence,
Affection and esteem.

DAVID HOPE

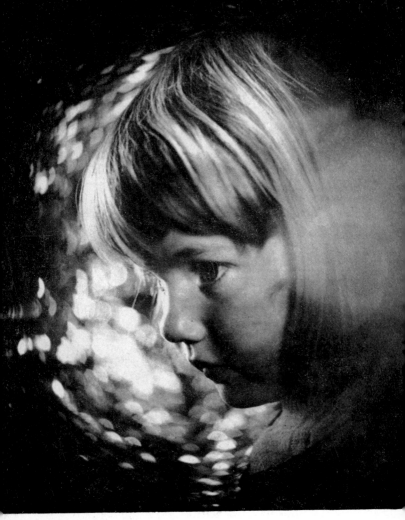

REVERIE

There is a secret wonderland
A child in dreams may roam,
Knowing that every path will end
Safely in love and home.

DAVID HOPE

THE FRIENDSHIP BOOK

DAME SYBIL THORNDIKE was talking to some school children about acting as a means of understanding others. She told of her school days when she sat next to a " horrid girl." Each evening she took to acting for her brother the events of the day in which her classmate was involved.

Gradually there came an understanding of the object of her annoyance as she imitated her more and more closely, entering into her feelings as she enacted the other girl's behaviour. Strangely, she came to find she no longer hated the girl.

In this way, said Dame Sybil, acting could lead to the imaginative study of others, of the pain that lies behind the stiffness with which a grandmother rises from her chair, of the weariness that governs the sharp answer of a mother. Through putting oneself in someone else's shoes can come sympathy and love.

SUFFER little children, and forbid them not, to come unto me : for of such is the kingdom of heaven.

AT a friend's birthday party last week, Jean, who's five, was asked if she would like another piece of cake.

" I would, thank you," she replied politely, " but I've had one slice already, and I'm just wondering if it's better to enjoy one slice than maybe feel sick after two slices !"

So young and yet so wise—though I'm happy to add, Jean *did* decide to have a second helping— and she *wasn't* sick !

THE FRIENDSHIP BOOK

DR AGGRI, a West African of Royal blood, was an expert on education. In the course of his work he travelled all over the world.

During a visit to Salisbury, in America, he died an untimely death.

Later, a tomb was erected above the grave, and on it was this phrase, a tribute by the American Ambassador to what was then the Gold Coast:

" He could be trusted absolutely."

Could there be a finer tribute?

THE groom was Olympic gold-medallist David Hemery. The bride was Irene, twin sister of Lillian Board.

David was previously engaged to Lillian, the Olympic silver medallist and winner of two European gold medals, who had died over three years before.

David and Irene, a social worker, were brought together through tragedy. Throughout Lillian's long illness, they had shared bedside vigils, and the constant strain of her last few months at the cancer clinic in Munich. They were both at her bedside minutes before she died.

Afterwards, David wrote a book on Lillian and her battle against cancer. He was greatly helped by Irene, both with the book and to get over the loss of the girl he'd hoped to marry.

After Lillian's death, David and Irene grew closer and closer. When they announced their engagement, both families were delighted.

The story that began in heartbreak had a happy ending—or a new beginning—in the sunshine of a spring wedding

THE FRIENDSHIP BOOK

I HAD a letter some time ago from Mrs Jean Noble, of Penicuik.

Jean, a nurse in a geriatric hospital in Edinburgh, wrote to tell me of two young relatives who became proud parents of a baby girl. She was their crowning joy.

Then, at six months, she fell ill. After tests, the doctors found there was nothing they could do. As gently as they knew, they told the young couple their baby could not live much more than a year.

Yet, because of mother's love and care, a year came and went, and then another. The baby grew to a toddler, and from a toddler into a lovely little girl. Her parents never stopped hoping for a miracle, though in their hearts they knew it could never be. And then, a few weeks before her third birthday, she died.

She was laid to rest in the cemetery at Lybster, in Caithness. And as Jean stood there in the cold and wet, all she could wonder was — why? Why did this little child, who had so much love to give and so much to receive, have to die, when in her ward in Edinburgh were others who, their lives over, longed to go, yet lingered on, suffering pain, loneliness, helplessness and sorrow?

It is a question to which there is no answer.

PERHAPS we say, " I'm sorry " when
  A thoughtless deed is done.
But stop to ask, " Now, could this hurt?"
  Before the thing's begun.
Be quick to help. To scoff, be slow.
A word or deed can injure so.

MAY

SATURDAY—MAY 1.

HERE is a story from Ireland which speaks of peace and beauty, from a young Paisley policeman for whom no spot can match a little haven in County Donegal.

It is the Tra-na-Rosaan youth hostel, on the Rosguill peninsula. Young folk from all over the world found their warmest welcome in Ireland, from the hostel's warden, Kitty McLoughlin.

Though no longer young herself, Kitty became the trusted friend of every youngster who ever went there. She sorted out problems, gave them advice, shared their hopes and dreams. She brought strangers together in friendships which will last a lifetime and in the evenings as the sun set, she held them enthralled with stories of her childhood and legends of old Ireland, told in her soft brogue. What is more, whenever a hosteller left, Kitty bowed her head and said a prayer for his safety as he travelled through her troubled land.

But when hostellers return to Rosguill they will find a stranger in her place, for Kitty has died. She was laid to rest in the little cemetery not far from the hostel, and I am told that the boys and girls who knew her will each spend a few minutes by her grave—trimming the grass, planting a wild flower or two, tidying the border or weeding the path—so, remote as it is, it will never be neglected.

How touched she would have been to know it.

SUNDAY—MAY 2.

O GOD, lift up thine hand: forget not the humble.

THE FRIENDSHIP BOOK

NOTHING stirs the interest of a congregation like the choosing of a new minister.

One congregation heard four applicants for the vacancy. The first was rejected because he was a bachelor, the second because he was over forty, the third because he was bald and the fourth because he wore glasses and read his sermons.

In despair the minister in the neighbouring parish wired a friend to take the service the Sunday after the abortive election. He so pleased the congregation that they unanimously elected him.

It was only after he had been settled a few months they realised he was a bachelor, over forty, growing bald, wore glasses and read his sermons!

TUESDAY—MAY 4.

IAN, who's seven, woke up at 3 a.m. one morning last week, calling for his parents.

His father went through to find out what was wrong. All the wee lad wanted was a light—he didn't like the dark. His father smiled. "Imagine a big boy like you being afraid of the dark," he scoffed gently.

"It's all right for you," said Ian reproachfully. "You've got Mummy to look after you!"

WEDNESDAY—MAY 5.

THE cost of living's pretty high—there's little
    free in life;
No end of things I can't afford, and neither can
    my wife.
How odd that things the most worthwhile (and
    they are very many) —
Health, sunshine, love, song and friends — just
    do not cost a penny.

HOW much do we know about our neighbours, their heartaches, struggles and burdens, or their successes and achievements?

The people who lived in the small town in Germany where he resided only knew Goethe, the great philosopher and writer, as a householder who regularly went for a walk every afternoon at precisely four o'clock. It was only when he died and his fame and world-wide reputation were broadcast in the newspapers that they realised they had had a great man in their midst.

The truly great are always the most modest.

FRIDAY—MAY 7.

WHAT prompts a poet to write a poem, or a composer a song?

One Saturday afternoon in 1946, a Scots boy was standing on the deck of a ship bound for Canada. Seeing his mother weep on the quayside, he shouted to her, " It's all right, Mum, we're no' awa' tae bide awa'."

These words haunted Ian MacPherson, who was near enough to hear them. That night, he sat down and wrote what is now one of Scotland's most famous songs :

> *Oh, we're no' awa' tae bide awa',*
> *We're no' awa' tae leave ye.*
> *For we're no' awa' tae bide awa',*
> *We'll aye come back and see ye.*

Now sung all over the world, Ian MacPherson would have been proud to know how popular his song had become. He died, alas, in 1965, aged 79, but his widow, Gwen, now over 80, felt that she had been left a tremendous legacy, one which will not diminish with the passing of the years.

THE FRIENDSHIP BOOK

SOMETIMES, 'twixt tea and sundown bright,
My little lad and I
Walk hand in hand in pastures green
Beneath a summer sky.
We walk and talk; and I, his Dad,
Just sheer enchantment find;
I marvel as his fresh, young thoughts
Pour from his lovely mind.
It seems to me the grass is sweet
For little, loving, happy feet!

I HAVE waited for thy salvation, O LORD.

SOMETIMES actions speak louder than words —and more effectively, too !

A friend living in Perthshire, tells me of an incident related to him by the Rev. Arthur Fletcher, of Newton Stewart. It's a true story of an eminent Scots doctor who, though not on duty, was driving through town a good deal faster than he should have been.

He glanced in his mirror and was dismayed to find that, right on his tail, was a police car. Quickly he reached into his case, took out his stethoscope and dangled it from the window—hoping, of course, the police would make allowances because he was a doctor.

The police car pulled out and drew alongside. The window wound down. And as the car sped past, the policeman in the passenger seat leaned out and dangled a pair of handcuffs, leaving a chastened doctor doing a modest 30 m.p.h.

TUESDAY—MAY 11.

WILLIE is always complaining.

To hear him, you'd think he was the hardest-worked, lowest-paid, most-exploited, least-understood man that ever was. So, despite myself, I groaned when I saw Willie coming my way the other day. I was in a hurry, and Willie was sure to delay me with all his complaints.

My first shock came when Willie smiled and grasped me firmly by the hand. I mumbled a greeting, and asked how his wife was.

" Marvellous, man, marvellous," said Willie. " After what she's been through it's a miracle she's alive. 'Course," he went on, " she's still partly paralysed, and her speech is a bit blurred, but she's still got her sense of humour."

I suggested we might have a cup of coffee, but Willie shook his head. " I'd like fine to, man," he declared. " But I must get the dinner on." Then he looked up at the sky. " With luck, I'll get the washing dry and the ironing finished before tea !"

And, with a wink and a wave of his hand, Willie the complainer was gone.

WEDNESDAY—MAY 12.

DID you know that Satan works for charity ? He has raised hundreds of pounds in aid of Lifeboat funds.

How do I know ? Well, Satan is the mynah bird in Pennan Inn on the north coast of Aberdeenshire. Above his cage is the R.N.L.I. collecting-box, and every time a coin is dropped in the box, Satan says, " Thank you." If he doesn't with the first coin, then it means that he wants another coin first !

Summer and winter, no one works harder for the Lifeboat service than Satan !

PALS

Large dog or small, it's all the same:
We want an outing and a game,
A master whom we can adore,
And, having these, wish nothing more.
Content like us, the human race
Could make the world a happier place.

DAVID HOPE

HOLIDAY MAGIC

Remember those days at the seaside?
The things we found on the beach?
The boats and the shells and the seaweed,
The bottle we couldn't quite reach?

What was it that made them so special,
Those days that we spent in the sun?
Looking back, we really did nothing,
But, oh, it was such super fun!

DAVID HOPE

CONTENT

We like our pond beneath the trees,
We like the pleasant summer breeze,
And as we cruise in search of food
We quack our thanks that life is good!

DAVID HOPE

THE FRIENDSHIP BOOK

YOUR house burns down, a loved one dies,
*   You lose a limb, we'll say,*
But how magnificent you are
*   On that disastrous day!*
And yet you fret, in panic get,
*   Because you lose ten pence,*
Or Jim comes late, Jane breaks a plate . . .
*   It simply won't make sense!*
Don't let life's little thing make you
A nervous wreck — they needn't do!

H. GARLAND MINTON, in his autobiography, "Blind Man's Buff," tells how one morning he was suddenly struck blind in the middle of a busy London railway station. He explained to a passer-by what had happened and asked him to fetch a policeman. The stranger assured him that he would do so; Mr Minton stood and waited, but no one came. The same thing happened with several other passers-by.

He was getting more and more desperate when one young voice answered him with such compassion that he knew at once that this time help would come. The young man expressed concern at the terrible thing that had happened, led him to a seat, and returned with a policeman in no time at all.

Mr Minton says he realises on looking back that all those others he asked for help were hurrying for their trains and probably thought what he said was too extraordinary to be true. Sad, isn't it, that many people who would like to help others, often hold back because they do not realise where the need is or how great it is.

THE FRIENDSHIP BOOK

SATURDAY—MAY 15.

THE Lady of the House was watching a TV play about Napoleon.

I was reminded of a story of one of Napoleon's soldiers, a boy of 19, found sleeping on guard duty and sentenced to death.

The day before his execution his mother went to Napoleon's headquarters to plead for his life. Somehow, she gained the presence of Napoleon himself. In silence he heard her plea. " Madam," he said, " do you think your son deserves mercy?" The little woman drew herself up and looked back at him fearlessly. " Sir," she replied quietly, " if he deserved it, it would not be mercy."

Impressed by her courage and dignity, it's said, Napoleon pardoned the boy. What is more, the soldier who slept on duty became one of his most brave and loyal men, until he fell in battle, giving his own life to save Napoleon's.

That, at any rate, is the story. Odd, isn't it, to think that a mother's love and a great man's forgiveness could be said to have changed the history of the world . . .

SUNDAY—MAY 16.

FOR thou, LORD, hast not forsaken them that seek thee.

MONDAY—MAY 17.

NOW, men who like to potter in
Their own small garden plot,
Are mostly friendly, modest chaps,
Who do not shout a lot.
I wish we had more gardens — then
There'd be a nicer race of men!

THE FRIENDSHIP BOOK

TUESDAY—MAY 18.

WHEN you sign a letter "Yours sincerely," do you know just what you've committed yourself to ?

Well, one explanation goes back to ancient Rome. When wealthy men bought marble statues for their gardens, some statue-makers weren't above using second-class marble which had cracks in it. They filled in the cracks with wax and when this was smoothed over no one could spot the difference. In time, of course, the wax melted in the sun, contracted in cold, &c., and the statue became cracked and unsightly.

So honest statue-makers put the two Latin words *sine cera*, meaning "without wax," on their orders, with their signature beside them as a bond. This came to mean a promise of honest and open dealing and, in English, *sine cera* changed to sincerely.

It's worth thinking about the next time you sign a letter !

WEDNESDAY—MAY 19.

IN his biography of Group Captain Douglas Bader, *Reach For the Sky*, Paul Brickhill tells a moving story of the time Bader was lying desperately ill in hospital after the plane crash in which he lost both legs. He heard very distantly a voice outside his room telling someone not to make a noise —"There's a boy dying in there." The shock of those words awoke in him a fierce determination to live and from that moment he fought his way not only back to life but also to become one of the R.A.F. heroes of the Battle of Britain.

A lesson to all of us on the power of determination.

THURSDAY—MAY 20.

IN a hidden corner of the grounds of Drumlanrig Castle, near Thornhill, in Dumfriesshire, stands a log summerhouse.

It has been there for many years. Few visit it now. It has been weathered by rain, wind and time. But you can still see dozens of initials carved into the wooden walls, posts and railings.

During the war, troops from Canada, Australia and New Zealand went to Drumlanrig to train for the Dieppe landings in 1942. For most of the men it was their first visit to the land from which their parents and grandparents had emigrated. The men grew to love the peace and beauty of Drumlanrig and, before they left, many went to the little summerhouse in the woods to carve their initials.

Those who recall the Dieppe landings will also remember the terrible casualties. Among them were many who spent happy months at Drumlanrig.

That's why today the log hut in that lonely wood stands as their memorial, in some ways more meaningful than a marble pillar on a hill top.

FRIDAY—MAY 21.

ON a cloudy day a boy was flying his kite, which had disappeared out of sight. A passer-by stopped to watch him and jokingly asked, "How do you know your kite is still in the air? I can't see it." "Neither can I," agreed the boy, and then, triumphantly, "but I know it is there. I can feel it pull."

How often we, too, may have felt the pull of the unseen when days are dark and we have almost lost hope.

THE FRIENDSHIP BOOK

SATURDAY—MAY 22.

A FINE tribute was paid to Robert Louis Stevenson when G. K. Chesterton said that he never let the smell of his medicine bottle get into his writing.

Blessings of value are passed on to us only from those who have received them in tears and pain. R.L.S. wrote to his fellow novelist, George Meredith: "For fourteen years I have not had a day's real health. I have written in bed, and written out of it, written in hæmorrhages, written in sickness, written torn by coughing, written when my head swam for weakness."

How many fine stories and poems the world would have lost had Stevenson passed his days being sorry for himself?

SUNDAY—MAY 23.

THE LORD shall endure for ever : he hath prepared his throne for judgment.

MONDAY—MAY 24.

JACK UNWIN has recently completed 50 years as a farmer. He began his work in Northumberland and later came to Lancashire, where his duties involved looking after 28 dairy cows and 400 head of poultry. In all his work with sheep, cows, bulls and poultry, he proudly claims that he has never once been involved in an accident.

Perhaps this is the kind of record boasted by many a farmer, but Jack is just a wee bit different.

He has been totally blind from birth.

Sometimes I think that if we are deprived of one sense, another one develops. Call it instinct or intuition, if you like. It isn't just luck.

TUESDAY—MAY 25.

H AVE you a friend who's not so well
In hospital or home —
Someone who loves the sunshine, but
No longer far can roam?
Drop in to see them for a while,
And share the sunshine of your smile.

WEDNESDAY—MAY 26.

TODAY I'd like to tell you about Grandpa Mac's Sunday ritual.

I can't give you his name, for reasons which will become plain, but he lives in Whitley Bay, and I'd like you to share part of his letter :

" Dear Francis Gay, old folk, with the best of intentions, are inclined to advise and sometimes interfere with the youngsters a bit more than we should, and many times are hurt by their reaction. I'm a grandpa, and have suffered in the past for my indiscretions by the reaction of my grandchildren.

" Then I found this prayer. I cut it out, and I read it every Sunday, taking its lesson to heart. As a result, I'm now much more welcome by the family. I know it would help many others, old and young, to get back on an even keel."

Lord, Thou knowest that I am growing older. Keep me from becoming talkative, and possessed with the idea that I must express myself on every subject. Release me from the craving to straighten out everyone's affairs and the desire to recite endless detail. Give me wings to get to the point. Seal my lips when I am inclined to tell of my aches and pains.

Make me thoughtful, not nosey; helpful, not bossy. With my vast store of wisdom and experience, it does seem a pity not to use it all; but Thou knowest, Lord, that I want a few friends at the end . .

THURSDAY—MAY 27.

OCCASIONALLY, I'm accused of being sentimental.

I used to find it a hard charge to answer. If I admitted it, I laid myself open to further charges that I live in a world of milk and honey, where the bad, the sordid, the rotten, do not exist. This is simply not true, of course. I doubt if many have seen as much of the other side of the picture as I have, or come up against more that is sad, harsh and cruel.

One day, I took down my dictionary and looked up the word " sentimental." I found the first part is from a Latin word, *sentio*, meaning " to feel." The second part would seem to be from another Latin word meaning "mind." Being sentimental simply means having a mind, or a soul or spirit, if you like, which can feel things, and be touched and moved by them.

If that is so, then I'm proud to admit to being sentimental. Aren't you ?

FRIDAY—MAY 28.

I SUPPOSE it all depends on the point of view, like the minister who said that when he came to his church he found it half empty and when he left it was half full.

But certainly the little girl saw things differently when her friend complained about the weather as it began to rain at the annual Sunday school picnic.

She pointed out, " But, don't you see ? It's God's way of watering the flowers."

The difference between a pessimist and an optimist is that one sees only the dark side and the other the bright side.

THE FRIENDSHIP BOOK

SATURDAY—MAY 29.

HERE'S a spot of sunshine, straight from the cheerful streets of Scarborough.

It comes to me from Mr J. Brown, of Newcastle. While he was in the holiday town, he saw a neat elderly lady, rather frail, standing at a kerbside, looking afraid to cross the busy street. A young policeman walked up to her, stood smartly to attention and saluted. Then he offered his arm. With a smile she placed her arm in his, he signalled with his other hand and the traffic stopped until they'd crossed safely.

On the other pavement, he again saluted and she gave a most grateful smile and a bow. Then they both turned and went off in opposite directions. Mr Brown couldn't help smiling himself and he remarked to the policeman, " That must be a Very Important Person, judging by the care and attention you gave her." The young policeman beamed. " Indeed she is a Very Important Person," he replied. " She's my mother."

Somehow, hearing of that little scene brightened my day.

SUNDAY—MAY 30.

JESUS himself stood in the midst of them, and saith unto them, Peace be unto you.

MONDAY—MAY 31.

*I*T *should have been so wonderful —*
Just my dear man and me,
Retired, with lots of things to do,
And lots of folk to see.
Now he is gone — yet how I bless
Those golden years of happiness.

HIGHLAND SENTINEL

A rugged, stubborn, splendid tree
Well suited to the land.
The roots hold firm among the stones,
A feeling in their very bones
All can understand.

DAVID HOPE

PERFECTION

You must have seen one sometime
No matter where you stay,
And it's always oh, so welcome
—A perfect summer's day.

DAVID HOPE.

JUNE

TUESDAY—JUNE 1.

A YOUNG couple who live not far from us had a worrying time lately.

Their little girl was ill in hospital. However, when they saw the care the nurses in the ward gave to all the wee ones, they knew she was in good hands.

One nurse in particular went out of her way to win the children back to health and strength. Every spare moment, she was playing with them, telling them stories or just cuddling them on her knee. As our young neighbour said, it's as if she loves them into getting better.

Two years ago that young nurse was married with a little boy. Then there was a tragic accident and the little boy was killed. A few months later, for no apparent reason, her husband left her.

Enough to crush the bravest spirit. But as soon as the worst of her grief was past, this young mother went back to her old job. " You'll not be wanting to go to the children's ward," said the matron. " Matron," replied the nurse simply, " it's the only ward I *do* want to work in."

There she is today, the nurse with the cheeriest smile and the quickest step.

WEDNESDAY—JUNE 2.

THE chores are done, the washing's out,
 The garden looks a treat;
Now for five blessed minutes I'll
Sit down and rest my feet.
Oh, what contentment just to be
An ordinary mum like me!

THURSDAY—JUNE 3.

WHAT a thrill it is for a granny to see her grandchild christened.

Mrs Gray, of Allanton, told me of one granny who couldn't get to her grandchild's christening service because she was in Hartwood Hospital, Lanarkshire. How disappointed she was!

But, instead of having her miss the service, the ceremony was held in the hospital ward.

The sun streamed through the windows, there were flowers around the ward, and the patients smiled happily. The baby's parents, his other grand-parents and his god-parents were all there. The minister, his wife and children, and even the church choir had come, too. There was quite a congregation, swelled by every nurse who could be spared.

What a moving service it was! Some of the old people had not seen a child christened for years, and they felt as proud as Granny when the precious bundle was placed in her arms.

There cannot be many babies who've been christened in a hospital ward. I'm sure that all who were there will never forget it.

FRIDAY—JUNE 4.

PAUL is as noisy as most five-year-olds. Indeed, his mother declares he's noisier. So much so that, at the height of a particularly trying day, she said to him, " For goodness sake, make less noise. My nerves just can't stand it."

That night, pink and shining after his bath, Paul knelt by his bed to say his prayers. " Please, God," said the small and serious voice, overheard by a listening mother, " either make me a good boy—or give Mummy stronger nerves !"

THE FRIENDSHIP BOOK

SATURDAY—JUNE 5.

A MAINTENANCE engineer of a TV rental company was called to Thatched House Lodge, Richmond, to service TV and stereo equipment.

The door was opened by Princess Alex herself.

"The servants are all out," she said, laughing at his startled expression. Then she led him to the room where the equipment was installed. The work took a little while, and it was well into lunchtime when the man finished. To his great surprise he was asked if he'd like to stay to lunch. Rather embarrassed at the idea of lunching at the Royal table he declined, saying he'd grab a bite in Richmond.

"Nonsense," said the Princess. "If you can make do with scrambled eggs, join me."

So saying, she donned an apron and whipped up two delicious platefuls of eggs, brown bread and butter.

This they ate, chatting over the kitchen table. A meal that electrician will always remember.

SUNDAY—JUNE 6.

I WILL not fail thee, nor forsake thee.

MONDAY—JUNE 7.

KIM HUBBARD may not be a familiar name in Scotland, but in America, from 1901 to 1930, she worked on the "Indianapolis News," and in its columns she created the sayings of Abe Martin. These sayings are amusing, witty, and well worth pondering. For example:

"When a feller says, 'It hain't the money, but the principle o' the thing,' it's the money."

Very true!

THE FRIENDSHIP BOOK

IN many parks in Scotland you'll find a monument to a Kilmarnock chemist.

George Forrest was born in Falkirk, and loved the open air. One day, out fishing, he found an old carved stone chest. He went to Edinburgh to learn more about it, met a professor from the Royal Botanic Gardens—and before he knew it, he had volunteered to go to China on an expedition in search of new plants and flowers!

He left in 1904. He didn't return until 1906, but when he came back, he brought with him the seeds of more than 5000 plants. He was to go on six more expeditions—to China, Tibet, Burma. He collected over 31,000 plants of rare beauty including blue poppies, primulas, gentians, clematis, and, his greatest love, rhododendrons, which came from a beautiful hidden valley in Tibet.

Despite dangers, hardships, sickness and disease, he battled on. He was still tramping the distant peaks when he died in 1932, and was laid to rest among the flowers he loved.

So when next you thrill to the sight of a rhododendron in full bloom, remember the humble Scot who left such a glorious legacy to us all.

SO I wrote a little letter
To a friend distraught with grief,
And the writing of that letter
Warmed my heart beyond belief.
Though my own heart had its sorrow,
Yet I shared another's load;
Lo, a miracle! That sorrow
Led us to a sunny road.

THE FRIENDSHIP BOOK

THURSDAY—JUNE 10.

IS our faith as strong as that of our forefathers a century ago?

David Livingstone, the famous explorer and missionary, was once stuck on the bank of a river for days, his native followers dreading to cross in such hostile territory.

Eventually he decided that the crossing would have to be made at night. In preparation for this, he opened his Bible, and the verse he read was, " Lo, I am with you alway."

He put down the book, and told his followers that they were going to cross the river at once. " What about the enemy?" they cried. " We will all be killed!"

" Jesus will be with us," he said. " He has promised to be with us always, and He never breaks his word."

The crossing was made without a casualty.

How good it is to be able to trust a higher power so completely with one's life!

FRIDAY—JUNE 11.

MRS GEORGINA HALL of Oldham sent me the following lines, and I thought you would like to share them with me :

When families celebrate it's like a holiday, and no one minds a formal room turned into disarray; a christening or a wedding feast, the family all unite in warm and happy comradeship, that breathes of true delight.

Yes, families are a bore at times, but if you were alone, you'd miss the greatest happiness you ever could have known; all family celebrations bring real warmth, and deep inside, a feeling of security and everlasting pride.

SATURDAY—JUNE 12.

IT sometimes seems as though film stars live in another world. But Gregory Peck has some thoughts on living which apply just as well to all of us ordinary folk :

"Living is loving what you do. You must be able to face the prospect of each day with concern and love for the people around you."

SUNDAY—JUNE 13.

I WILL both lay me down in peace, and sleep : for thou, Lord, only makest me dwell in safety.

MONDAY—JUNE 14.

"MELITA" is the name of a house in West Road, Fraserburgh. It is a name that has puzzled many strangers to the town, but the local people know its origin, and why it's there.

For twelve years this house has been the home of two remarkable ladies, Miss Watson and Miss Wood. Between them, until they retired in 1962, they spent over 100 years in charge of fishermen's missions at Peterhead, Milford Haven, and Fraserburgh. There, fishermen far from home could relax over a cup of tea, find a warm welcome, and someone to listen to their troubles.

Often Miss Watson and Miss Wood had to break the news of a tragedy at sea to the men's wives and families. None knew better the dangers our fishermen face. That's why they called their house " Melita " —for it is the tune of the fishermen's hymn " Eternal Father, strong to save."

When Miss Wood died, at 82, that hymn was sung at her funeral. Surely a fitting farewell to one who did so much for those in peril on the sea.

TUESDAY—JUNE 15.

ISAAC WATTS was a young grumbler—one of those critical young men who grumble loudly. He grumbled about the hymns sung in church and complained Sunday after Sunday until his schoolmaster father was driven to say, " Well, go and do better yourself."

He did, many times ; once with " Oh, God, our help in ages past " and another time with " When I survey the wondrous Cross."

Now if only we could all turn our grumbling into such inspired channels !

WEDNESDAY—JUNE 16.

GOD bless all sick folk everywhere,
And all who suffer pain,
All invalids, all crippled folk,
And all who long have lain
In bed by day and night, and know
How wearily the hours go.

THURSDAY—JUNE 17.

AN old friend calls himself " seventy years young." I asked him his secret and he smiled. " When I was young I used to worry a lot. One day somebody to whom I confided my worry said, ' What were you worrying about ten years ago ?'

" ' Don't be daft,' I replied. ' How can I remember ?'

" ' Well,' he said, ' ten years hence you won't remember what you're worrying about today.' "

There is a Golden Day in every week. Yesterday we can do nothing about, for it is past. Tomorrow is still to come. But today is ours to do with what we like. Live for the Golden Day.

FRIDAY—JUNE 18.

IN the absence of the Lady of the House I was boiling an egg for myself with a time-glass to keep me right. As the sand trickled from one compartment down to the other, I recalled how an hour-glass used to be put on the edge of the pulpit to time the minister's sermon.

If the sermon was boring, how eagerly the congregation would watch the trickling of the sand, but sometimes, if he was in good form, the preacher would simply turn the glass over and continue preaching!

Time never passes more slowly than when we watch it, and never more quickly than when we forget it.

SATURDAY—JUNE 19.

ALL our life is a time for reaping, not one day should go by when we do not store some experience for the future. Perhaps some gladness of true friendship to warm our heart, some new meaning of love and beauty, or some new strength gained by overcoming difficulty.

We know that Dr Albert Schweitzer's work at Lamberene was halted during the Great War, because he was deported and interned in France; but the great man soon began to learn how to reap experience for the future from this unaccustomed situation into which he had been plunged. He put his time there to good use. He made friends, who were later able to help him in his work, and he committed to memory the beautiful Bach fugues that brought to him a new meaning of love and beauty. From this music he loved, he gained a new strength which enabled him to overcome apparently insurmountable difficulties.

THE FRIENDSHIP BOOK

SUNDAY—JUNE 20.

SALVATION belongeth unto the Lord; thy blessing is upon thy people.

MONDAY—JUNE 21.

ENOCH POWELL, the well-known politician, became an atheist when he was in his twenties. In the book he wrote, *No Easy Answers*, he describes how, many years later, right out of the blue, he went and sat in a church one Sunday evening. This was for him the beginning of a way back to a belief in religion.

He says that at first he was almost afraid to think too deeply about it in case his new-found faith should come to an end. But gradually he found " I would no more need to fear coming to the end and walking out empty-handed than the scientist needs to fear getting to the bottom of the natural universe."

Mr Powell is a man who holds some controversial views, but this is one with which we can all agree wholeheartedly.

TUESDAY—JUNE 22.

I WAS passing down an unfamiliar street the other day when from some derelict buildings I heard the shouts and laughter of children. Curious, I went over to see the source of their amusement.

Where once a garden had been, there was still a patch of grass and on it children were kneeling and making daisy chains from the flowers which starred the ground.

The little daisy plot in the centre of the busy city gladdened my heart. It seemed to take me back to a simpler, uncomplicated world.

WEDNESDAY—JUNE 23.

AS we left the local drama club's production, we agreed that one lady of our acquaintance, with a small part, had excelled in it.

A friend, who had heard an extra special compliment to her performance, began to say, "Well, I don't know if I should tell her or not——"

"Of course you should," said an old lady who happened to overhear her. "People are only too glad to pass on bad reports, why not pass on good ones as well?"

Why not give a pat on the back when it is deserved? Everyone likes to receive compliments.

THURSDAY—JUNE 24.

WE have all heard the story of the Good Samaritan of the Bible, but how many know about the man who came to be called the Good Samaritan of Gallipoli?

He was Private John Simpson of Durham. John Simpson was one of the stretcher-bearers who in 1915-1916 regularly traversed Shrapnel Gully, the highway between the beaches of Gallipoli and the front line. The Gully got its name from the ceaseless shelling with which the Turkish forces bombarded it. He discovered a donkey nearby, and together they delivered wounded men to the safety of the dressing station on the beach.

In 24 days, this ordinary man, who scorned both reward and personal safety, saved many lives —no one knows just how many. Then, as was inevitable, a machine-gun bullet ended his heroism.

A stone on his grave is inscribed: "He gave his life that others may live."

Who could wish for a finer epitaph!

THE FRIENDSHIP BOOK

FRIDAY—JUNE 25.

IT'S no use pretending the sky's always blue,
That life's just a beautiful song;
Clouds often arise, and for me and for you
The shadows of sorrow lie long.
If we're to keep on we must somehow grope through
The darkest and stormiest night,
Assured that, with courage and faith, we'll come to
A day that is sunny and bright.

SATURDAY—JUNE 26.

NOT long ago a Dundee businessman went on a bus tour.

There was much to see, for the countryside was at its loveliest, but the most vivid memory he brought home was not of hills, woods, or fields, but of watching the party in the bus singing " The Bonnie, Bonnie Banks o' Loch Lomond."

And I do actually mean " watching," for most of the people in the bus could neither hear nor speak.

A feature of most bus trips is the sing-song on the way home, at the end of a happy day and this one was no different, for the folk in the bus " sang " on their hands !

Together, in perfect unison, they spelled out the words of all the old favourites on their fingers, keeping time and capturing the rhythm just as they would if they'd been singing it. Not only " Loch Lomond," but " Ye Banks And Braes," " Auld Lang Syne " and many more—and, judging by their smiles, they enjoyed the songs every bit as much as you and I might do.

A silent song, perhaps, to those who listened. But what glorious melody the singers heard in their hearts !

E

THE FRIENDSHIP BOOK

THE fool hath said in his heart, There is no God.

I AM proud to pass on this challenging story. A successful Glasgow businessman, now retired, lost his wife after 37 years of happy married life.

He'd been a bit of a gambler, and one night soon after they were wed, he lost nearly £100 at cards—money entrusted to him by his firm. Next morning, shattered by what he'd done, he poured out the story to his wife. "If I put it back by tonight it'll never be noticed," he said. "But how can I? I've nothing!"

When he came in at midday, his wife handed him an envelope containing £96. "Here," she said, "I saved this from the housekeeping." That day, he paid it back. No one ever knew the truth.

Oddly enough, neither did he, until a few days before his wife died. One evening, as he sat by her bed, she asked him to fetch her jewel case. Mystified, he did so, and she took out her engagement ring. Then she told him that, all these years, she'd lived with a lie. The money she gave him hadn't been saved. She'd sold her engagement ring back to the jeweller, and bought a cheap imitation diamond which she'd worn ever since. "I knew you'd never notice," she smiled. "Besides, our happiness meant more to me than any diamond. I hoped I'd never have to tell you, but now you must know the truth."

In those last few days, that cheap glass ring drew them closer together than ever, and now it is a husband's most cherished reminder of the wife who built a lifetime of happiness around it.

TUESDAY—JUNE 29.

> *LORD, bless my son, though far away;*
> *And, if it be Thy will,*
> *Protect him from all dangers, and*
> *Whate'er might do him ill.*
> *Oh, bless my boy, good Lord, and bring*
> *Him safely back to me;*
> *And may he know each night that I*
> *Commend him unto Thee.*

WEDNESDAY—JUNE 30.

MIDWAY in his preaching career the Rev. John Watson, D.D., better known as Ian Maclaren, the author of *Beside the Bonnie Brier Bush*, was suddenly attacked by lung trouble and forced to rest for six months. Particularly he had to rest his voice, a considerable trial to one accustomed to using his in the service of others.

He and his wife took a holiday in Europe and Egypt and made plans to deal with the necessity of keeping silent when travelling by train. Mrs Watson was to make one remark to show that they were " happy, 'though married "; then, if the fellow-traveller was a German, Dr Watson was to listen and from time to time gently clear his throat. When the fellow-traveller was a Frenchman he was again to listen and at the end to smile and give a one-word assent.

The difficulty lay with English-speaking holiday-makers, delighted to find a fellow countryman to whom they could talk. Again he listened and listened. He found that he learnt a great deal and at the same time he gave to a lot of people pleasure and relief. He " gathered the harvest of a quiet tongue," and he performed the ministry of silence.

Everybody loves a good listener !

JULY

THURSDAY—JULY 1.

SIR ARCHIBALD McINDOE, the plastic surgeon who did well-nigh miraculous work in restoring the faces and hands of terribly burned airmen during the last war, was also very concerned to keep up the spirits of his patients.

Once when a visitor remarked on the relaxed and happy atmosphere of the hospital, Sir Archibald replied, " But I am making faces. What is the good of making them if they do not set in happy lines ?"

Perhaps we who have the choice could set our own faces in happy lines more often than we do ?

FRIDAY—JULY 2.

JACK ASHLEY was a Member of Parliament on the threshold of an outstanding political career when he became totally deaf.

Although his first reaction was to resign, he was encouraged by his wife, friends, constituents and other politicians to learn to lip-read and carry on his duties as an M.P. In later years he was to say:

" The depths of human affection and kindness are not plumbed without a crisis. Deafness has given me a profound appreciation of my family and real friends; an insight into the unrecognised humanity of the House of Commons; a knowledge of despair and hope I would never otherwise have known and a greater understanding of my fellow man."

And, we might add, an ability to count his blessings in no small measure.

SATURDAY—JULY 3.

A JOB'S to be done or a duty performed,
  But you're scared of the terrible minute;
You're sure you will fail—yet the big thing to do
  Is to make up your mind to begin it.

Turn coward, postpone, lose your nerve—and no doubt
  There will come a black day when you'll rue it.
Get cracking at once, and keep on with a grin,
  And I'll bet my last penny you'll do it!

SUNDAY—JULY 4.

O LORD our Lord, how excellent is thy name in all the earth !

MONDAY—JULY 5.

AS children, how we enjoyed the fairy tales of Hans Christian Andersen! He wrote in his autobiography, " Life itself is the most wonderful fairy tale," and he spent his, making children happy.

Very often the stories he wrote did come from his own life. But, being a dreamer, he saw how beautiful life might be as well as how drab it sometimes was. His mother's sad tale of being sent out to beg when a child, and of her shame and fear of going home empty-handed, he turned into the moving beauty of " The Little Match Seller." His story of the ugly duckling emerging as the beautiful swan has given encouragement to many youngsters who saw themselves as the " ugly ducklings " of their own families.

We need practical people to get the daily work done, but how dull life would be without dreamers like Hans Andersen.

THE FRIENDSHIP BOOK

TUESDAY—JULY 6.

A CERTAIN American business man found it easy to write angry letters, but discovered that it wasn't so easy to say the same thing when he met the person face to face.

" The trouble is," he said, " when you meet the other fellow he's such a darned nice guy!"

WEDNESDAY—JULY 7.

VERY few people in this country have heard of Kate Marsden, yet in parts of modern Russia she is famous. For in the 1890's this trained nurse and dedicated Christian began to inquire into the lot of lepers in Russia. Armed with a letter of introduction from the Princess of Wales, she personally interviewed the Empress of all the Russias and learnt of the lepers of Viluisk, expelled from their homes to a living death in the frozen forests of Siberia.

Kate Marsden went to see for herself, enduring terrible hardships on the journey which were to leave her an invalid for thirty years. What she saw made her badger the Russian authorities until, six years later, a leper hospital was built.

That same hospital was closed down not so many years ago because, thanks to one determined woman, there are now no more lepers in Viluisk.

THURSDAY—JULY 8.

H OW pleasant when you chance to meet
*   Somebody with a smile;*
It makes the sun light up the street,
*   And brightens every mile.*
If someone's smile can help you through,
Please smile at folk when they meet you!

NOW IT'S GONE!

Bubbles are fun to blow, but teach
That pride precedes a fall:
As bursts each rainbow-coloured globe
There's nothing there at all!

DAVID HOPE

TIMELESS

I love those secret places
Where peace comes dropping slow,
And the sky looks down each dawning
On the unchanging scene below.

DAVID HOPE.

FRIDAY—JULY 9.

MANY years ago the Rev. John Brown of Haddington was riding through Tranent, in East Lothian, on a horse which was going lame.

A man who was known to be an agnostic called out in mockery, " Doesn't the Bible say, ' The legs of the lame are not equal '?"

The minister had an answer ready.

" Aye," he called back. " In Proverbs, Chapter 26, it says, ' The legs of the lame are not equal; so is a parable in the mouth of fools ' !"

SATURDAY—JULY 10.

THE Queen Mother was coming to open the new wing of the college and all was in readiness for her arrival. The principal was to welcome her at the gates where she would alight and walk through the grounds.

A group of nursery-school children had been given a special place to one side of the gates, so that nothing could block their view, and the excitement was great when the Royal car was seen approaching.

It was followed by dismay, for the Queen Mother was sitting on the other side. When she stepped out she would be completely hidden from small viewers by the large car until she disappeared within the college walls.

But, quickly grasping the situation, that most gracious Royal visitor stepped past her lady-in-waiting, who was sitting beside her, and smilingly alighted on the " right side," to the great delight of the children.

The truly great always have time to think of others.

SUNDAY—JULY 11.

BEHOLD, the fear of the Lord, that is wisdom; and to depart from evil is understanding.

MONDAY—JULY 12.

I HAVE seen loneliness in all its shapes and forms, and how it can affect a person. And sometimes there isn't a thing I or anyone else can do about it, because of five little words, which almost guarantee loneliness: "I keep myself to myself."

I was reminded of all this by a letter from someone who'd heard these words spoken by a neighbour last week. "I know she's very lonely," said the letter, "and I wish I'd had the courage to tell her friendship is a two-way thing, and that you've to go halfway to meet it." How true, and it's failure to realise this which makes "I keep myself to myself" one of the saddest sayings of all.

Remember:

I went out to find a friend; a friend I could not see.
I went out to be a friend; and friends just flocked to me.

TUESDAY—JULY 13.

THE famous actor, Edmund Kean, once recited the 23rd Psalm to a roomful of people, who applauded the perfection of his diction and delivery. Noticing an aged clergyman present, Kean asked him to repeat the psalm as he thought it should be read.

When he had faltered to a close the great actor, deeply moved, declared, "I read it as if I knew the psalm, but he read it as if he knew the Shepherd."

THE FRIENDSHIP BOOK

MAKE straight your back, your shoulders square,
It only takes a minute,
But that's the way to face a day
That has some sorrow in it.
Press on with hope, your head held high,
Ev'n though dark clouds blot out your sky.

THURSDAY—JULY 15.

I DON'T suppose many people noticed.

On the first Saturday of the Glasgow Fair she was up early, and when she drew her curtains she saw neighbours off on holiday, waving happily as they left.

It reminded her of the days when she and her husband and family went off to Dunoon or Rothesay. So, after breakfast, she made sure her pensioner's concession ticket was in her purse and took the bus to one of Glasgow's busiest bus stations.

Not because she wanted to go anywhere, but just to stand in the queues where she could listen to people's plans and get caught up in the children's excitement. When the bus arrived she slipped away and joined another. Sometimes to make the dream last a little longer she boarded the bus, too, and used her pensioner's ticket to go a mile or two on its way. Then, back to the bus station and another queue.

Later that day it all became too much for her. She had a dizzy turn and was taken to Glasgow Royal Infirmary. There the whole story came out to a sympathetic nurse, who, moved and saddened by her loneliness, told it to me.

In years to come the Glasgow Fair will always recall that small, grey figure in the bus queue.

THE FRIENDSHIP BOOK

A PRESENT from Butlins with a difference.

Nan and George White and their 10-year-old twins, Ann and Gillian, went on holiday to Butlins for a week. There they met Mr and Mrs Hume from Cumbernauld. From the very beginning the two girls were attracted to the old couple. They, in turn, were touched at the way the twins seemed to take to them. Then they learned that their grandparents had died before the children were born. When Ann and Gillian heard their friends talk about visits to grannies and grandpas they wished they, too, had them. So they told their mother to ask Mr and Mrs Hume if they'd be their granny and grandpa. They were too shy to ask themselves!

Well, of course, Mr and Mrs Hume were delighted, and Ann and Gillian were simply thrilled. Already they've had postcards from their new grandparents. They've had a week-end visit from them, and the twins gave them breakfast in bed. And they're discovering that all their friends had told them about grandpas and grannies being somehow special is very true.

In an age when family relationships so often seem to take second place, this story gladdens my heart.

IT'S, " May I have this?" and it's, " Can I do that?"
    And, " Please may we go out to play?"
My goodness, from morning till evening those kids
    Are round me the whole blessed day!
When prayers are said and they're snuggled in bed,
    A kiss on each unfurrowed brow,
I sigh as I turn out the light, and I wish . . .
    I wish I'd been kinder, somehow.

THE FRIENDSHIP BOOK

SUNDAY—JULY 18.

I HAVE esteemed the words of his mouth more than my necessary food.

MONDAY—JULY 19.

ON an old bookmark appears the following short poem :

Think truly, and thy thoughts shall the world's famine feed;

Speak truly, and each word of thine shall be a fruitful seed;

Live truly, and thy life shall be a great and noble creed.

—So simple, and yet so profound !

TUESDAY—JULY 20.

A CLIMBING friend was asked recently to accompany a lame botanist up a mountain. Knowing the dangers and difficulties of the climb, he agreed with some misgivings, and the twosome set out to climb up to the dangerous gully where the flower the botanist sought might be found.

The botanist was quite inexperienced, and his thoughts were only of the flower he longed for. He did things no climber would have dared ; with thoughts only on his goal, he climbed steeps experience would have pronounced unclimbable, unwittingly caused his companion untold anxiety, and ended with a cry of delight, safe at the top of the precipice where his treasure was found in abundance.

In some mysterious way his simple single-mindedness had kept him safe.

How often success is achieved by forgetting about the difficulties in our path !

WEDNESDAY—JULY 21.

A VERY foolish fellow he,
  Who with childlike delight
Says, " I don't worry, folk, because
  Whatever is, is right."
And foolish also he whose face
  Is always sad and long
Because there's nothing anywhere
  That isn't wholly wrong.
The truth lies somewhere in between,
  If rightly understood;
Our job's to bear life's ill with grace,
  And thank God for the good.

THURSDAY—JULY 22.

I HAVE just heard of a young man lying very ill in hospital.

Although he was in much pain, he forced himself to speak cheerfully and look bright when his wife, Mary, and family came to see him.

To his mother, he wrote:

" Mum, I don't know any words that could express the way Mary has kept me going. I'd have given up a long while ago if it hadn't been for her. The way she has nursed me through pain, comforted me, lifted me out of depression and made me carry on when all I wanted to do was pack up because of the seeming futility of it all has been marvellous.

" For me to have been off work in pain for six months is bad enough. For my Mary to have stood that, yet look after the boys, manage the house and go out to work to help out our money, makes her nothing less than a saint in my eyes."

Which of these takes the more courage? The husband who knows the end is near? Or the wife who must soldier on? I doubt if anyone can answer.

FRIDAY—JULY 23.

AN American publisher once printed one of Robert Louis Stevenson's books without permission. That was bad enough. But what made R. L. S. even more furious was the fact that his name had been misspelt. " I saw my book advertised as the work of R. L. Stephenson, and I own, I boiled. It is so easy to know the name of a man whose book you have stolen, for there it is full length on the title page of your booty. But he . . . he calls me Stephenson !"

Our name is a precious part of our identity, and the sound of it conjures up an image. We cannot all be gifted as R. L. S., but we can make sure that the image that our names create in others is one of goodness and loving kindness.

SATURDAY—JULY 24.

NO one was there to meet him from school, the poor little fellow. Only six he was, blind in one eye, and he had a limp. Knowing that the lad also suffered from St Vitus's Dance, his teacher decided to follow him at a discreet distance to see that no harm came to him on his way home. Stopping at a corner to peer down at the pavement, the lad saw her, and told her furiously he did not need help.

Such was that boy's determination to succeed in life that some seventy years later, when he was buried in Westminster Abbey, all that was needed to mark his grave was a simple stone bearing the inscription—*Samuel Johnson.*

SUNDAY—JULY 25.

AND having food and raiment let us be therewith content.

THE FRIENDSHIP BOOK

BROKEN hearts can be hard to mend, but Lizzie Aitken, of Greenock, knows the secret. It all began in 1894 when she was given an accordion. She was only ten, but it didn't take her long to learn to play it, and soon feet were tapping merrily to her music.

Then Lizzie got married and, with a house to look after and a family to raise, the accordion was put into a cupboard and almost forgotten.

In 1939, Lizzie's husband died and left her a widow at 55. Cleaning out the cupboard one day, she came on the accordion, dusted it down, and tried it out. Finding that the old magic was still there, Lizzie started to go out again. She played for old people, the housebound, even at concert parties.

Never a week passed without the accordion being used somewhere, and the remarkable thing is that Lizzie and her squeeze-box are still on the go. Now over 90, she says, " It's grand to see old folk enjoying themselves !" And the young folk, too, for I'm told she took her accordion along to her great-great-granddaughter's wedding and was the pride of the gathering.

Lizzie's accordion has helped her to find the greatest secret in life. If you want happiness for yourself, you've got to give it to others.

*Y*OU wish that you'd a garden
    To grow a flower or two,
Then when you visit shut-in folk
You'd take them round a few?
Nice thought! But chatting for an hour
Can mean as much as any flower.

FOREIGN LANDS

The whole world's at your finger-tips,
Choose any stamp you please
And take imaginary trips
To lands across the seas.
It's quite the most attractive way
In which to learn geography.

DAVID HOPE

LOOKING UPWARDS

To dwell beneath hills is to feel
That life has a greater dimension
Than houses and streets can reveal
To our all-too-restricted attention.

Who raises his eyes to the heights
  Can witness a pageant unending
That offers more lasting delights
  Than a lifetime of getting and spending.

DAVID HOPE

PASSING HOURS

The man who strikes the bell
　　Stands ready night and day;
His duty is to tell
　　That time is on its way.
Ours is to use it well
　　In making history.

DAVID HOPE

WEDNESDAY—JULY 28.

A CHINESE proverb was sent me recently from Hilda Holmes, of Wythenshawe, Manchester. It says:

If you keep a green branch in your heart a singing bird will lodge there.

You may say this is a pretty thought, nothing more. But surely this saying—centuries old—reminds us that if misfortune or bereavement comes into our lives, and we allow these to make our heart cold and dead, we shall suffer still more. But if we are brave enough to keep an interest in things, count our blessings and smile bravely in an unkind world, we shall find happiness, and hear a little bird singing every day!

And this is profoundly true.

THURSDAY—JULY 29.

WHEN an officer failed in his duty during the American Civil War, President Abraham Lincoln's Secretary of War, Edwin M. Stanton, was so furious that he said to the President, " I'll sit down and give that man a piece of my mind."

" Do so," replied Lincoln. " Write it while you have it fresh in your mind. Make it sharp. Cut him all up."

The War Secretary at once sat down and wrote a crushing letter, reading it out to President Lincoln, who said, " That's a good one—it's fine."

" Whom shall I send it by?" queried Stanton.

" Send it?" came the reply. " Don't *send* it. Tear it up. You have freed your mind on the subject and that is all that is necessary. You never ought to *send* such letters. I never do."

Try that with *your* grievances. Put them on paper—and then tear them up and forget about them.

FRIDAY—JULY 30.

LIFE seemed so grey six months ago,
All hope, she sighed, had gone;
So many troubles that there seemed
No point in going on.
But yesterday we met—and she
Was bright and cheerful as could be!

SATURDAY—JULY 31.

THE man who wrote this letter lives in Airdrie. To spare his self-respect I'll use only his first name, Andrew. He says :—

" People don't think those two little words, ' thank you,' exist any more. They can bring happiness to almost everyone. Yet try it, and you're often laughed at as some kind of nut !

" When I was younger I, too, thought I was Jack the Lad. Open a door for anyone? You must be joking ! Say thanks for a favour? You're not on !

" I was far too concerned to get what I wanted to think of saying thanks. With much shame I remember the time I borrowed some money from a girl friend's elderly parents, who could scarcely afford it. But I never thought of saying thanks, let alone returning it.

" But now I'm older and wiser, I think of them only with embarrassment and shame. If I could put things right now I would—if only to end the tormenting thoughts I keep getting over them. But I doubt if they'd care very much now, and who could blame them?

" If you should show this letter to anyone, try to make them realise there's an awful lot of happiness to be got from two little words.—*Ex-sailor, officer and (rather late) a gentleman.*"

AUGUST

HE knoweth the way that I take.

EVER heard of Rent-A-Mum?

Four years ago, Mrs Billie King, 5 Bolton Grove, Hartlepool, lost her husband. She tried to pick up the threads, but the one thing she missed was someone in the house to care for. Then she came across Rent-A-Mum—a service providing temporary mothers for families whose real Mum is ill, in hospital, on holiday, &c. It was just what Mrs King needed — and she loved her new job.

While helping out with a family near Selkirk, she did everything a Mum does—washing, ironing, cooking, taking children to school, shopping, drying tears, tucking in at night, telling stories, sharing secrets and listening to prayers. Only one thing she couldn't do—go to church. She'd tried, but she found it too upsetting.

Then she had a word with the minister at Ettrick. He explained others had faced the same problem. " Just ask God to help you through the service," he said. " Somehow, He will."

And He did—in an unexpected way! When the collection was being taken, instead of putting his penny in the plate, the youngest of her three charges—aged two—tried to take a £1 note out! Of course, Mrs King had to smile, and at that moment all her anxiety seemed to drain away. As the service ended, and the wee lad fell asleep in her arms, she knew she'd never be afraid to go to church again.

F

Tuesday—August 3.

DAG HAMMARSKJOLD, who was Secretary-General of the United Nations until his tragic death in an air crash in Northern Rhodesia in 1961, looked at life with profound simplicity.

We must live one day at a time, he maintained:—
" Do not look back. And do not dream about the future. It will neither give you back the past nor satisfy your other daydreams. Your duty, your reward—your destiny—are *here* and *now*."

Wise words for these worrying times.

Wednesday—August 4.

*M*Y *goodness, sir or madam, I*
Can find no end that's wrong.
And so can you—such ills and cares,
Such fears that linger long.
But don't lose sight of what is bright—
And thank the Lord so much is right!

Thursday—August 5.

THE indomitable Mrs Rose Fitzgerald Kennedy, whose life has seen so much tragedy and suffering, wrote her memoirs at the age of 83. Talking about her grandchildren, she said :

" I hope they will have strength to bear the inevitable difficulties and disappointments and griefs in life. Knowing that tragedies befall everyone, and that although one may seem singled out for special sorrows that is not really so ; that worse things have happened many times to many others in the world and that it is not tears but determination that makes pain bearable."

That Mrs Kennedy could write such words must be an inspiration to us all.

FRIDAY—AUGUST 6.

WATCHING a very polished show on TV one evening, I was reminded of a story told by the BBC producer, Howard M. Lockhart, of that evergreen star, Gracie Fields.

She was top of the bill in one variety show Howard was producing, and he was surprised to see her getting more and more agitated as it came nearer her turn to go on.

" You're not nervous, are you?" he asked.

" I'm petrified !" she replied. " You see, when you are on a pedestal it's easy to be toppled off !"

I would go so far as to say that we are all on pedestals of various heights, and though perhaps we haven't so far to fall, I hope we all try as hard as Gracie did—to keep on our own small pedestal of self-respect.

SATURDAY—AUGUST 7.

IN vain, visitors to Geneva's Cathedral of Saint Pierre look round for the tomb of John Calvin. Arriving from France at the age of twenty-seven, John Calvin preached there for thirty years, and made such an impression that what had been a frivolous city, given to disturbance and riots, became a place of study, prayer and faith, and a refuge for those seeking religious freedom.

There are tombs and monuments to noble and Royal worshippers, but of Calvin only the bare, humble seat on which he sat in the pulpit.

This is no accident. It is as Calvin wished. He wanted to be buried as a humble citizen in the graveyard of Plainpalais—with no stone, no relic that might make visitors think of him and not of God, even for a moment. All thoughts were to be of God. " Soli Deo Gloria."

SUNDAY—AUGUST 8.

WHILE the earth remaineth, seed time and harvest, and cold and heat, and summer and winter, and day and night shall not cease.

MONDAY—AUGUST 9.

LEARNING to be penitent is not easy, but when a young novice nun, St Therese of Lisieux, was reprimanded by the mistress of novices who saw a broken vase on the floor at her feet, she accepted the rebuke and kissed the ground in penitence, although she had had nothing to do with the accident.

A Hindu friend told how her father used to scold whichever of his daughters was nearest when some misdemeanour came to light. She did not resent this, for, as she so truly said, " Any of us *might* have done it."

" There, but for the grace of God, go I."

TUESDAY—AUGUST 10.

A SCOTTISH lassie who went out to Africa as a missionary worked in a little place miles from anywhere, seeking to teach the Africans of God and Jesus Christ and His great love. One man would listen with interest to everything she said except when she spoke of religion. At last she said to him, " You are a father, and I know you love your children. What would you do if you called one and he refused to come?"

" Why," he answered, " I should speak so gently to him that he would want to come."

" Exactly," she replied, " that is what I mean to do with you until I bring you to the Great Father who is calling you."

THE FRIENDSHIP BOOK

WEDNESDAY—AUGUST 11.

THE task seems quite impossible,
Far, far too big for you;
You know it's quite beyond you, and
A job you'll never do.
But have a go—and here's the thing
That thousands have proved true—
You CAN do the impossible,
And do it finely, too.

THURSDAY—AUGUST 12.

TED was on a coach travelling between New York and Florida. On the same bus was a bunch of young people, as lively as Ted was silent. When the bus stopped at a restaurant, everyone except Ted got out for a snack. The youngsters realised that Ted had not got out and took him a sandwich. Then his story began to come out.

He had just been released from prison after serving a five-year sentence. He had written to his wife, but had not received a reply to his most recent letter, and did not know whether she would have him back.

However, he had asked his wife in his last letter, if she still loved him and wanted him home, just to tie a ribbon to the big tree in the centre of the little town in Florida to which he was now travelling. At that moment Ted was very unsure of himself and the reception he would get.

But the young people got excited for him and looked for the tree. Ted found himself much too nervous to do so.

What a cheer went up when the tree eventually came into sight, absolutely covered with ribbons of every size and colour !

The prodigal was welcomed home—and knew it.

FRIDAY—AUGUST 13.

IN a quiet country churchyard in Newland, Gloucestershire, lies the grave of George Morgan, who died in 1770. On his headstone are the simple words :

Say more I need not, and say less who can;
Here lies a generous, humane, honest man.

I don't think anything more needs to be said, do you?

SATURDAY—AUGUST 14.

"I AM fond of a cup of tea with a bun; and, with the bun you can give me a piece of cake. Busy as usual, I see, with the pots and pans; and if I may add, with the spoons and knives and the new bronzes on the mantelpiece and the walls."

This odd collection of words will mean little to most people, but a great deal to a few. They are the opening lines in Exercise 5 of the " Primer in Standard English Braille," a step in the patient learning of Braille by the blind, and by a host of transcribers who turn recipes, hymns, knitting patterns, plays or newspaper articles into Braille for their use.

Miss Ivy Williams, a barrister, who learnt Braille when threatened with approaching blindness, compiled this brilliant primer.

It is a real thrill to see a blind reader singing away from the sheets of the morning hymns Brailled for her use.

So—I am fond of a cup of tea with a bun.

SUNDAY—AUGUST 15.

THOU shalt make thy prayer unto him, and he shall hear thee.

THE SKETCHERS

Tomorrow's architects, maybe,
Learn from a great tradition
Whose daring and integrity
Must fire them with ambition.

DAVID HOPE

HARVESTERS

There's always work on a farm to do
   And it's never too soon to begin,
Toiling away the whole day through
   To bring the harvest in,
Making a youngster tall and true,
   And tanning his healthy skin.

DAVID HOPE

THE FRIENDSHIP BOOK

MONDAY—AUGUST 16.

"GO placidly amid the noise and haste, and remember what peace there may be in silence. As far as possible, without surrender, be on good terms with all persons. Speak your truth quietly and clearly; and listen to others, even the dull and ignorant. They, too, have their story."

This quotation came from a paper found in Old Saint Paul's Church, Baltimore, dated 1692.

Nearly three hundred years later we can still appreciate the wisdom of these words.

TUESDAY—AUGUST 17.

AMONG my acquaintances is a little man—a draper—who is one of the most ineffective and pathetic figures I know.

He lost his wife many years ago, and his two sons and one daughter, all married, have not been near the old home for I do not know how long.

He is still serving behind the counter of his little, dimly-lit shop, and his profits must now be very small. The last time I saw him he looked thinner than ever, and all his conversation was a whine against fate.

" If only things had been different . . ." he complained, and I remember him using that same phrase many years ago.

I mention him because he is an extreme example of what happens if all we do in life is to complain about things being as they are. All of us would like something to be different—taxes lower or wages higher, or a bus route altered. And who is to blame us ? We are permitted a comfortable and occasional grumble against such things. But year after year to go on complaining — why, that's just suicide.

Don't you agree ?

THE FRIENDSHIP BOOK

SOMEONE you trusted lets you down,
And oh, what pain is there!
Such faith you had, such confidence,
And now, just mute despair.
But, friend, in spite of all the tears
And heartbreak it has cost,
The one who thus betrayed you is
The one who truly lost.

THURSDAY—AUGUST 19.

THREE cheers for the teddy bear with the flashing eyes!

He stands about 18 inches high. He's just the kind of cuddly teddy every toddler loves, but there's more to this particular teddy—a lot more.

In his tummy, in place of the usual squeak, there is a little microphone, a miniature amplifier, and a battery just like the one I use in my transistor radio. Wires from the amplifier lead up to a pair of little bulbs behind the teddy's eyes.

A complicated teddy, but he and other bears like him are doing an amazing job. For they are helping deaf children to speak! How do they do it? Well, whenever you say anything to him, his eyes begin to flash.

Children love to see this, of course—and I'm told that deaf toddlers soon realise the way to make teddy's eyes flash is to speak to him. Once they grasp this, their speech apparently comes on by leaps and bounds.

The man who invented this remarkable bear, Ron Power, has devoted his life to helping the deaf. And I'm sure he had his reward with the first word prompted from the first child by the first teddy bear.

THE FRIENDSHIP BOOK

D'YOU remember the story of the little boy who called to his father from his darkened bedroom?

" What's wrong?" asked Dad. " Nothing," said the little voice, " I just wanted to know there was somebody there!" I was reminded of the story by this letter from a widow :

" Since my husband died," she wrote, " I have lived alone, and I have found great comfort in the lighted windows of my neighbours in the dark evenings. If I feel a bit lonely I have only to cross the road for a chat and a cup of tea.

" Lately I haven't been sleeping well, and the other night I saw the light on in the early hours of the morning. Just then the ambulance drew up and my neighbour's husband was taken away to hospital. I went over and felt I was able to help her just by being there, sharing a cup of tea. I know the awful feeling of an empty house, with one's dear one in hospital. I'm so glad I was awake that night."

Just to know there is someone there, someone who cares, is what counts, whether you are a wee boy who fears the dark, or a lonely widow.

ENRICO CARUSO, the Italian tenor greatly admired for the beauty of his voice, was also dearly loved for his personal qualities. His wife, Dorothy, in her story of his life, tells how one day when he was signing cheques for the two hundred or so people he helped to support, she murmured, " Surely all these people aren't deserving?" And he replied, " You are right, Doro, but can you tell which is and which isn't?"

What a generous way of looking at things !

THE FRIENDSHIP BOOK

THOU wilt shew me the path of life: in thy presence is fulness of joy; at thy right hand there are pleasures for evermore.

THESE days there are many folk who have lost their faith in the power of prayer. Perhaps they should remember James Hudson Taylor, who launched a campaign in 1865 to found a mission in the interior of China.

His method was to pray for missionaries to be called to the job, and for their expenses to be met, and then to wait for God to supply them. When Taylor died in 1905 the China Inland Mission had more than 800 missionaries stationed all over that vast country.

More things are wrought by prayer than this world dreams of.

GRACE DARLING, the heroine of the Longstone Lighthouse, off the Northumberland Coast, was 22 when she made her perilous journey through the storm to save the lives of others. It seems tragic that at the age of 27 she died of tuberculosis. Her frailty and her suffering emphasise the courage of this young girl. She had a weak body, but a valiant and faithful soul.

Each of our lives is always long enough for the tiny part of this world's work assigned to it. Not one of us can make excuses for an unfulfilled life. The span of time here on earth is never too short if every minute of it is filled with simple faith and love.

THE FRIENDSHIP BOOK

SOME people might complain, but don't;
They suffer pain, yet smile.
They get more than their share of knocks,
Yet go that second mile.
By keeping on, the brave find out
There's still so much to sing about.

I SUPPOSE you could call this a sermon, yet to Mrs Carmichael of Lennoxtown, it began as a simple incident during another day's work in a children's ward in hospital.

One of the patients was Jimmy, a boy with serious paralysis of the spine. Mrs Carmichael had just passed round the lunch trays, Jimmy's included, and popped back into the ward kitchen to fetch the meal. She'd scarcely left the ward when she heard a loud clatter, a tray falling to the floor. She whisked back, and, sure enough, Jimmy's tray lay by the side of his bed.

Now Mrs Carmichael who has an unconscious habit of knitting her brows in a frown when worried or displeased, picked it up without saying a word, but Jimmy noticed her frown and as she turned to leave he beckoned her back. With tears in his eyes he looked up at her—and this is what he said : " When I'm a big woman like you and you're a wee boy like me I'll not look at you like that."

Of course, Mrs Carmichael made light of her frown and gave Jimmy a quick hug. But when she got back to her kitchen she found a most unprofessional tear in her own eye.

Sadly, Jimmy passed on soon after. But Mrs Carmichael tells me she hasn't frowned since !

ONE may see in a picture what is hidden from another's eyes. So I can appreciate the incident of two men who were studying the painting of a harbour scene in the National Gallery.

One remarked to his friend, pointing out the fishermen idly sitting or strolling about, " That picture should be called ' Micawber '—waiting for something to turn up."

" Oh, no," replied the other who had noticed the mended nets and the prepared boats, " don't you see? They have done everything they could, and are waiting for the turn of the tide."

There are times when we have done what we could and there is no more we can do but wait for the tide to turn. It always does, you know.

A ONCE popular song contained the words, " Little things mean a lot." How true! Here are some of these " little things " :

The smallest crust may save a human life;
The smallest act may lead to human strife;
The smallest touch may cause the body pain;
The smallest spark may fire a field of grain;
The smallest deed may tell the truly brave;
The smallest skill may serve a life to save;
The smallest drop the thirsty may relieve;
The slightest shock may make a heart to grieve.
Nought is so small that it may not contain
The rose of pleasure or the thorn of pain.

AND God said, Let there be light : and there was light.

THE FRIENDSHIP BOOK

MONDAY—AUGUST 30.

NOW Tommy's caught the measles,
And wee Susie has the flu.
John's away for two whole weeks—
What can a mother do?
A cheery knock, a friendly call—
" I've made a cup of tea!"
God bless the neighbour who has time
For a harassed mum like me!

TUESDAY—AUGUST 31.

A FRIEND of mine spent a week sailing off the west coast of Scotland with his family.

They explored little hidden inlets and they saw splendid sunsets, but one of their most unforgettable memories is of the day they visited Fingal's Cave, on the Isle of Staffa.

It was a perfect day. The sea was calm and they were able to land without difficulty. The splendour of the soaring stone columns above them almost overwhelmed them, and they fell silent with wonder. Most awe-inspiring of all, from within came a vast, continuous thunder, almost as if a tumult raged there. Gingerly, they made their way towards it.

They reached the back of the cave to find no foaming torrents, no crashing waves—but simply ripples breaking gently on a little shingle beach! It seems the shape of the cave amplifies even the smallest sound a thousand-fold.

In a way, it's like fear, trouble and disappointment. At first there appears no way to rise above it. It is too big for you, and you know it. Yet by pressing on you may find that the boulder which blocks your way is no more than a pebble on the path.

SEPTEMBER

EDITH DAVIDSON, of Aberdeen, sends me this story.

A teacher friend has the unenviable task of sorting out whose shoes are whose after a gym lesson, and making sure they're all fastened up.

One day, she'd helped 25 five-year-olds to lace up 50 small shoes, with seven more children to go. As the teacher struggled to her feet after finishing wee Susan's, the little girl looked up, wide-eyed, and said, " Please, miss, these aren't my shoes."

The teacher sighed. Down she went on her knees once more, unlaced them, and took them off again. " Now, Susie," she said patiently, " if they're not yours, can you tell me whose they are ?"

" Yes," said Susan innocently. " My big sister's —but Mummy says they're too small for her now, so I can wear them !"

SURELY a dentist's chair is the last place you'd expect to find a parable.

Yet that's where a friend of mine came across one. He'd an appointment to see about a new set of dentures. Of course, there was the usual rigmarole, taking impressions, and so on.

Then the dentist brought out a small tape measure—and asked my friend to smile ! " Why ?" he asked, mystified. " Because if I know how wide your smile is," the dentist said, " it will help me to do a better job on the dentures."

That tickled my friend immensely. Especially these words : " A smile helps me to do a better job."

How does your smile measure up ?

THE FRIENDSHIP BOOK

FRIDAY—SEPTEMBER 3.

ONLY one place at the table to set,
Only one coat on the hook;
One pair of slippers to warm by the fire,
Only one dinner to cook.
When my Jim died I knew fine there would be
Changes one never foresees;
Lord, I can cope with the big ones, all right,
But give me the courage for these . . .

SATURDAY—SEPTEMBER 4.

I RECEIVED a letter from a Liverpool fireman not long ago.

He signs himself simply " K. R.", and encloses this poem he wrote, which he and his mates sent in memory of the seven Glasgow firemen who died in the tragic warehouse blaze a few years ago, and as a tribute to all firemen who daily face danger and death :

He stands on the stairs with the flames licking round—a child to be saved, an old dear to be found; he thinks of his own children, safely in bed, then takes a deep breath and goes on ahead.

His heart's beating faster, the fire's gaining hold; up the next flight, he must try to be bold; he hears someone screaming and bumping around —somebody's trapped, by the flames they are bound.

Nearly there now, but it really is hot; his smoke-tortured lungs are tied in a knot. He makes a quick search where he thought he heard sound, finds a tiny limp body to be got to the ground.

Now he himself can hardly get breath, gives his mate on the ladder the child, saved from death. But, alas, underneath him the floorboards give way, and a fireman's own kids lose their father that day.

SUNDAY—SEPTEMBER 5.

LO, I am with you alway, even unto the end of the world.

MONDAY—SEPTEMBER 6.

CHARLES KINGSLEY, the novelist, was once staying in a home where there was a little girl. The day on which he was leaving was dark and dismal, and as he was about to go, the little daughter of the house said to him : " Mr Kingsley, will you please write something in my autograph album ?"

Kingsley looked up at the dark skies and shook his head, but the little girl pleaded with him. So the great man took up his pen, and this is what he wrote :

My fairest child, I have no song to give you,
No lark could pipe to skies so dull and grey;
Yet ere we part, one lesson I can leave you
For every day.

Be good, sweet maid, and let who will be clever,
Do noble things, not dream them all day long,
And so make Life, Death and that vast For Ever
One grand sweet song.

TUESDAY—SEPTEMBER 7.

IT happened in the days when railway passengers were segregated into three classes.

The ticket inspector came up to one traveller who happened to be in a second class compartment and confessed that she thought she had got into the wrong carriage. The inspector said sternly, " The difference in the fares must be paid."

"Good !" said the passenger, triumphantly. "Then I'll trouble you for 3s—I've a first class ticket."

WEDNESDAY—SEPTEMBER 8.

HEAVEN is a plot by my back door,
  Just twelve feet six by nine,
Where I can potter happily,
  And sit out when it's fine,
Or pick a flower or two to share
With those bowed down by grief or care.

THURSDAY—SEPTEMBER 9.

PYTHAGORAS lived 500 years before Christ. He was a great mathematician and every schoolboy knows his famous theorem. But he is remembered for other things, too. He believed we should see God wherever we look. He has been quoted down the ages for his protests against cruelty to animals and his belief that God is The Spirit permeating the Universe, from whom everything that is born takes its life.

One story about him is that he would go down to the seashore market and buy fish alive just so that he could have the pleasure of immediately returning them to the water. We may not all agree with everything Pythagoras taught, but we must all admire a man who holds so firmly to his principles.

FRIDAY—SEPTEMBER 10.

THOMAS CARLYLE'S first love was Margaret Gordon, but she was not allowed to marry a poor schoolmaster, and in her last letter to him she wrote :

" Genius will render you great. May virtue render you beloved. Remove the awful distance between you and ordinary men by kind and gentle manners."

Good advice for any famous person, then, or now !

G

THE FRIENDSHIP BOOK

EVER heard of Gingerbread?

Of course you have! It's the stuff that makes the kitchen smell fragrant, and disappears almost as soon as Mum brings it out of the oven.

But I'm speaking of another kind of Gingerbread which, in its own way, brings another kind of fragrance to kitchens all over the land. It began when an unknown young woman was left on her own with two young children to bring up. She struggled on, but sometimes the odds seemed all against her.

Then one day, as she sat weary and depressed in a London coffee bar, she began to think of others like herself, left alone with children to raise, and no one to turn to. If only they could all get together, to cheer each other up, to help each other with advice, to share ideas, or even just to chat for a while.

The more she thought about it, the more she was determined to do something about it. And she'd call the club " Gingerbread," after the coffee bar where the idea first came to her.

Today, throughout the country, there are more than 150 Gingerbread groups. Anyone who is left to bring up a family alone is welcome to join. And though no one knows now where the girl who started it has gone, her idea has brought happiness and hope to thousands.

Yes, I like the taste of the Lady of the House's gingerbread. But I like the sound of the other Gingerbread even better!

CAST me not off in the time of old age; forsake me not when my strength faileth.

THE FRIENDSHIP BOOK

ENJOY yourself on holiday,
Wherever you may be,
In busy streets or countryside,
On hills, or by the sea.
But spare a thought and prayer today
For all those who at home must stay.

BECAUSE of the mosquito-infested swamps and the difficult terrain, the digging of the Panama Canal was a formidable task. It could not have been accomplished without the courage and determination of the labourers.

It was also due to the spirit with which they tackled the job. Each workman, for example, had in his bunk a plan of the completed canal as an aim towards which to strive. Even more they became inspired with what came to be known as The Panama Song;

If you have rivers they say are uncrossable,
Or mountains you cannot tunnel through,
We are specialists in the wholly impossible,
Doing the thing that nobody can do.

THE age of innocence is still with us, thank goodness !

I'm reminded of this by an incident which I heard about recently. A little girl of three was taken aside by her father, and told proudly that a new baby brother had arrived just one hour earlier.

Little Karen's eyes shone, and she clapped her hands. " Daddy," she cried, " can I be first to tell Mummy ?"

THURSDAY—SEPTEMBER 16.

I'M indebted for this story to the baker's vanman.

It seems a bobby on his beat saw a man with a penguin waiting in the bus queue. He learned the man had simply found it. When asked what he planned to do with it the man confessed he had no idea. " Well," suggested the bobby helpfully, " why not take it to the zoo ?" " Good idea," said the man, and off they went together.

Next day, the same policeman was amazed to meet the same man, still with the penguin. " Look here," he said, just a wee bit annoyed, " I thought I told you to take that bird to the zoo ?"

The man nodded. " I did," he beamed. " And he enjoyed it so much I'm taking him to the circus tonight !"

FRIDAY—SEPTEMBER 17.

HAVE you heard of Macpherson's Law ?

You may remember, it gets the blame for all the awkward happenings because Macpherson's slice of toast always lands with the jammy side down. Yesterday, I came into the kitchen to find Mrs Gay pouring what looked perfectly good sugar into a tin for throwing out. She explained she'd mixed salt into the sugar container, and put it down to Murphy's Law.

" Surely you mean Macpherson's ?" I queried. " Oh, no, Murphy's." I wondered how they differed. It seems Murphy's Law states : If anything can happen it will. I confess I didn't see much difference. Then it was explained to me that Macpherson accounts for awkward happenings only. Murphy allows for the good things that can come about as well as the bad.

Trust a woman to go one better.

THE FRIENDSHIP BOOK

THIS is the story of Granny McAllister's pilgrimage. She began in 1965 and has tramped hundreds of miles. Although she's well over 70 now, she plans to keep on as long as she can.

Intrigued? I'm sure you are, especially when I tell you Granny McAllister's pilgrimage takes her not to the Holy Land, Lourdes, church or chapel—but to eight pubs in Glasgow's Cowcaddens.

Every Thursday night at half-past seven, she wraps up warmly, picks up her brown shopping bag, and sets off from her home to start her rounds.

In the shopping bag is a collecting tin, and when she pushes open the door of the Variety Bar and pulls out her tin, she's met with smiles and good-natured banter. But the regulars never let her down, and soon she's off to the Kiwi, the Loughwilly, and another five pubs in the area. In each she's welcomed with warmth and affection — and pity help anyone who's less than a perfect gentleman while she's there.

On Friday night she's back again, and on Saturday, too. She's never home until after ten. But in her years going round the pubs, I'm told she and her tin have raised thousands of pounds for pensioners—to give them a treat now and then; to buy a bag of coal or two; to make sure none is forgotten at Christmas.

That's the story of the pilgrim in the pub. To me, Granny McAllister's pilgrimage is as brave as any I've read about in the history books.

IN Thee, O Lord, do I put my trust : let me never be put to confusion.

THE FRIENDSHIP BOOK

IT has been called the song the whole world sings.
Not a single day passes, but it is sung somewhere. It has been played by the greatest orchestras and sung by the greatest choirs in the world. It is heard in palace and in cottage.

Before I say what it is, I'd like to tell you about two sisters, Mildred and Patty Hill, who lived in Kentucky. Patty became a nursery school teacher, Mildred, a music teacher. Both devoted their lives to children from poor homes.

For them, the sisters composed little songs. Patty made up the words, Mildred, the tunes. Every day the sisters sang " The Good-Morning Song " to the children—and the children sang it back to them :

" Good morning to all, good morning to all,
Good morning, dear children, good morning
    to all !"

And if any of the wee ones had a birthday, the words were changed slightly, though the tune remained the same. Yes, that schoolroom song, written more than 75 years ago is " Happy Birthday To You !"

Mildred, who died in 1916, never knew how popular it would be one day. But Patty, who lived until 1946, saw it become the birthday song of the world.

A FRIEND you have not seen for years
    Comes back and grips your hand,
And leads you off to yesterdays
    In childhood's fairyland.
What memories you two can share
In that escape from daily care!

LEARNING

I'm helping Granny with her spinning.
It's hard to do at the beginning,
But in a while I'll learn the knack
And Granny then can just sit back!

DAVID HOPE

REFLECTIONS

My mistress thinks me such a pet. It's true
I like my comforts and I'm glad to play.
Wouldn't she be astonished if she knew
Outside I am a tiger, stalking prey!

DAVID HOPE

THE FRIENDSHIP BOOK

JEAN GORDON, of Perth, went for a run to
Pitlochry one summer day last year.

She drove to Bridge of Cally, then took the
road across the moors to Moulin. A few miles
from Kirkmichael, she passed the gates of Black-
craig Castle—two massive stone pillars, each
surmounted by a carved stone bloodhound.

She tells me that once an English tourist passed
these same gates, and decided to pull the leg of
the old lodge-keeper who was working in the
garden beside them. " My man," said the visitor with
a lofty smile, " how often do you feed your dogs ? "

Without batting an eyelid, the old man replied,
" Only when they bark, sir ! "

YOU will search the catalogues in vain for a rose
called Frank Reynolds.

But the Lady of the House and I have one in
our garden—a remarkable flower which opens to
a bloom of purest yellow, becomes tinged with
pink in a day or two, then, by the time the bloom
falls, has turned to the deepest crimson.

Its true name is Masquerade, but it was a gift
from Frank many years ago and we call it by his
name still. Frank is dead now, but his rose always
reminds me of him and of a sermon in five words
he once shared with me in a letter from his home
in Loughton :

Faults. Husband. Quarrel. Wife. Faults.

I confess it had me puzzled at first, until Frank
explained what it meant. Simply that, in a quarrel
between a husband and wife, there are usually
faults on both sides !

Neat, isn't it ? And true.

FRIDAY—SEPTEMBER 24.

KNOW what a disco is?

It's a dance, usually for young folk, where the music is supplied by records played through high-powered amplifiers, accompanied by spectacular lighting effects.

A young friend who visited a disco in West Regent Street, Glasgow, recently had a great night.

Scores of youngsters, mostly in their teens or early twenties were dancing in time to the music. Yet the astonishing thing is, most of them didn't hear a single note, despite the volume at which it was played!

Why? Because they are deaf. And if you're wondering how on earth they could dance to music they could not even hear, here's the explanation. In a disco, I'm told, some of the lights flash in time to the rhythm of the music that's being played. What is more, the vibrations travel through the air and floor, and the dancers can pick them up that way. So, though the youngsters cannot actually hear the music, in a way they can see it and feel it, well enough to be able to dance to it!

Every month, this disco for the deaf brings young people not only from Glasgow, but from miles round about, and I'm told many a romance has flowered there, too.

Yes, even though a world is silent, there can still be magic in it!

SATURDAY—SEPTEMBER 25.

NO trouble keeping cheery
When life is like a song.
A very different story
When things just go all wrong.
It's hard to smile — yet if you do,
Your clouded sky will turn to blue.

THE FRIENDSHIP BOOK

GOD be merciful unto us, and bless us; and cause His face to shine upon us.

JAMES NASMYTH, the Scottish-born engineer, invented the steam-hammer at his Bridgewater foundry at Patricroft near Manchester.

One day, the Emperor of Russia sent an equerry to James Nasmyth to inform him that he proposed to visit his works next day. The proprietor replied that they would be closed, the next day being Sunday.

The messenger tried first to bribe him by promising a large order from his master, and then, failing, said with a sneer, " If your Queen asked, you dare not refuse."

Nasmyth was down upon him like one of his own steam-hammers : " Her Majesty is a Christian lady, and would not tempt me to disobey the King of all kings, nor to deprive my work people of their Day of Rest."

Truly a man of principle.

YOU'RE as young as you feel !

I'm reminded of this by the story of a lad who, at 14, started work on a farm as a shepherd's boy. He served three generations of the same family, and at length, after 65 years on the same farm, his employer suggested gently that it might be a good time to retire. After all, he was now 79.

But John was deeply offended. " Huh !" he retorted, " if I'd known the job was just temporary, I'd never have taken it !"

THE FRIENDSHIP BOOK

IT'S some time since I visited Selkirk, but it's a friendly town I've always liked, so I'm not surprised by this story.

Between six and seven most evenings, you might see a figure hurrying through the streets bearing a large message bag. She is a nurse, and she's on her way to begin night duty.

What's in the bag? Well, if you peeped inside, besides her knitting and a few magazines to help pass the time, you'd find a loaf of bread, a pot of home-made jam and half a pound of butter!

Sometimes, you see, patients wake up during the night. When that happens and provided there are no problems about diet, out come the loaf, the jam and the butter, and the patient is handed a cup of tea and a jammy slice of bread. "You can't sleep if you're hungry," says the nurse.

Some people declare medicine these days is in danger of losing the human touch. But so long as we've nurses who believe in the magic of bread and jam, I don't think we need worry too much!

JANE is nearly four.

After breakfast the other day, her father rose from the table, said good-bye, then stooped and kissed her. "Good-bye, Daddy," Jane replied—then, gravely lifting her napkin, she wiped her cheek.

Daddy pretended to be hurt. "Wiping away my kiss, dear?" he chided. Jane looked up at him with a smile of beguiling innocence.

"No, Daddy," she said. "I'se rubbing it in!"

It's never too early for a woman to begin twisting a man round her little finger!

OCTOBER

RATHER pleasant to look back over the years to a tragedy, and smile.

Well, perhaps it wasn't a tragedy. It began one summer day soon after the Lady of the House and I were married. In a small shop we saw a beautiful little decanter and three goblet-shaped glasses, all etched with quaint scenes. We bought them for a song, and were very excited about the purchase. We didn't know a thing about glassware, but as it happened we had picked up a bargain.

A year later, at spring-cleaning time, the Lady of the House carefully washed the glassware in soapy water and I dried all of them except one of the three tumblers. It smashed in my hand.

That was the tragedy, if you like to call it that. But now, long years after, we never see the decanter and the two glasses without a smile, thankful neither of us said unkind things to the other, or blamed the other, when I broke that third glass.

That means more to us now than any glass could ever have meant.

THE name of the Very Rev. Dr Walter Chalmers Smith, who died in 1908, doesn't mean anything to most people now. But it was he who wrote that inspired hymn, " Immortal, Invisible " chosen by Princess Anne for her wedding service.

All laud we would render; O help us to see
'Tis only the splendour of light hideth Thee.

Someone once called it " the hymn that makes the sun shine." Long may it continue to be sung.

THE FRIENDSHIP BOOK

LET patience have her perfect work, that ye may be perfect and entire, wanting nothing.

MONDAY—OCTOBER 4.

WHEN Bob Edmonston emigrated to America as a young man, he became a civil engineer, and for years dreamed of bringing water from the north of California to the parched deserts of the south. Many experts ridiculed Bob's plan for a giant aqueduct.

But Bob persevered. As the years passed, others began to see that what they'd once thought impossible could in fact be done.

He never lived to see his dream come true, as he died in 1957. But today his aqueduct carries millions of gallons of water to Southern California where thousands of acres of desert are now fruitful, wildlife flourishes and the danger of drought is gone. Indeed, it is one of the biggest engineering projects ever, and I'm told that astronauts on the way to the moon saw only two man-made objects— the Great Wall of China and Bob Edmonston's aqueduct.

I doubt if you'll ever want to build an aqueduct —but in the parable of Bob's impossible dream there's surely a message for all who dream dreams.

TUESDAY—OCTOBER 5.

YES, times are bad and won't, I fear,
    Improve for quite a while;
But every day's a challenge, friend,
    To spread around your smile.
For friendship, kindness, humour, too,
Will help us see this battle through.

WEDNESDAY—OCTOBER 6.

TRANSLATORS of the Bible sometimes experience difficulty in translating words and phrases, familiar enough to us, into the idiom of peoples in other parts of the world.

Dr Harold Moulton was thus engaged in translating into the Eskimo language the words "There shall be much joy in the presence of the angels over one sinner that repents." He struggled to find a suitable Eskimo word to express "joy." Then he observed an Eskimo dog vigorously wagging its tail as it relished a delicious bone—and Dr Moulton had his word.

Translated back into English, his Eskimo translation read: "There shall be tail-wagging in the presence of the angels over one sinner that repents."

THURSDAY—OCTOBER 7.

TWO young girls agreed to take part in a parish visitation, but when they made their first call they felt so tongue-tied and embarrassed that they decided to pay no more visits.

The following Sunday the householder who had been visited went to the vicar after the service and told him, "I had a call from two young girls last week. They were so shy and nervous they hardly said a word. But after they had gone I couldn't stop thinking about their disappointed faces as they went away."

The stranger went on, "It came to me, Vicar, that if those two girls had the courage to do that for the church it was time that I was doing something. So I've come to begin again."

Sometimes, what we take to be our failures, unknown to us, become our greatest successes.

FRIDAY—OCTOBER 8.

WHICH is the real you? Edward Sandford Martin asked that question of himself in the following lines :

Within my earthly temple, there's a crowd ;
There's one that's humble, one that's proud,
There's one that's broken-hearted for his sins,
There's one that, unrepentant, sits and grins.
There's one that loves his neighbour as himself,
There's one that cares for naught but fame and pelf;
From much corroding care I would be free,
If once I could determine which is me.

SATURDAY—OCTOBER 9.

GRANNY MACKENZIE'S home was in Greenock.

She had lived there for many years, and during her last illness, all the family came to take their leave of her. One of the last to see her was her youngest granddaughter, who arrived with the husband she'd married only a few months earlier. Granny smiled a welcome and chatted for a few minutes.

As they rose to leave, she pointed to a photograph on the wall beside her bed of herself, aged 20, and her husband on their wedding day. " Aye," she said, " it's a long time looking forward, but it's no' so long looking back . . ." Then she added softly, " Remember, the secret is never to waste a single minute in between."

What more precious legacy could there be for a young couple on the threshold of life?

SUNDAY—OCTOBER 10.

WHAT is man, that Thou art mindful of him ?

THE FRIENDSHIP BOOK

MONDAY—OCTOBER 11.

IN an old Suffolk churchyard can be seen this epitaph to a schoolmaster :

"The body of Lewis Webb, schoolmaster, like the cover of an old book, its contents worn out, and stripped of its lettering and gilding, lies here.

"Yet the work shall not be lost, for it shall (as he believed) appear once more in a new and most beautiful edition, corrected and revised by the Author."

TUESDAY—OCTOBER 12.

HOW'S your faith in human nature ?

Mrs Ruth Currie, 25 Aytoun Road, Glasgow, tells me her brother has sold his caravan. A couple came to look at it, liked it, agreed to pay the £325 he wanted, and drove off, towing the caravan behind them.

An hour later, Mrs Currie's brother counted the money and, shocked, found he was £100 short. All he knew was the buyer's name, and that he lived near Johnstone. But off he went, drove round for two hours, and had to return without finding the caravan or the man who'd bought it. A bit of a shaker, frankly. The man had seemed to be so friendly and decent.

Two days later, the phone rang. It was the man who'd bought the caravan. He explained he'd been working nights. He'd just got home and put on his Sunday suit. To his horror, he'd found £100 in his pocket, and realised it was part of the caravan money. He wanted to hand it over as soon as possible.

Of course, he needn't have. But he did.

How's your faith in human nature now ?

WEDNESDAY—OCTOBER 13.

WHEN all alone you'd sit and weep
For one you love, now gone;
A little voice within your heart
Bids you to soldier on.
How great the cost, none but you know,
As with your memories you go.

THURSDAY—OCTOBER 14.

HOW do you break the news to someone that something they've treasured all their life is, in fact, of little worth?

This question faced Michael Low, who has an antique shop in Blanefield, near Glasgow. An elderly woman had written from Glasgow asking if he'd like to buy a silver teaset.

Well, Michael found her in a tenement in Maryhill. The teaset had been her mother's proudest possession, and she, too, had always treasured it. But now she had to sell it. She'd been told it was worth £150—and she needed the money.

But as soon as Michael saw the teaset he knew it wasn't silver, but cheap plate, worth only about £20. Well, Michael broke the truth to her as tactfully as he possibly could.

Instead of being upset about it, however, she smiled with relief. " You see," she explained, " if it had been worth £150 I would *have* to have sold it. But if it's only worth £20—well, I could never sell it for that . . . and so I'll be able to keep it." She paused and stroked the teapot with a gnarled hand. " It would really have broken my heart to have parted with it," she added.

Michael didn't get the teaset—but he found that sometimes treasures are all the more precious for being worthless, if you see what I mean.

FRIDAY—OCTOBER 15.

DURING a visit to Edinburgh in 1865, the great singer, Jenny Lind, called at a shop in Princes Street to buy some songs, and the young man who served her, not knowing who she was, asked whether she had heard the famous Jenny Lind.

" Yes," said the lady. " Have *you* heard her?"

" No," replied the young man. " I should very much like to do so, but unfortunately I cannot afford to go to the concerts."

The customer then asked the young man if he would be good enough to play the accompaniment of a song which she had chosen. She sang the song right through, and never had the pianist heard anything so beautiful.

When she had finished the song she smiled to him, " Now you *have* heard Jenny Lind."

SATURDAY—OCTOBER 16.

HAVE you ever doubted or feared? Have you ever faltered or failed? All of us, at some time or another, surely have. And that is why all of us can take heart from these lines sent to me by Mrs Helen Campbell, of Pine Street, Kingston, Ontario. Mrs Campbell, now nearing 80, has come a long road, and this verse frames the philosophy of a lifetime :

Who never wept, knows laughter but a jest;
　Who never failed, no victory has sought;
Who never suffered, never lived his best;
　Who never doubted, never really thought;
Who never feared, real courage has not shown;
　Who never faltered lacks a real intent;
Whose soul was never troubled, has not known
　The sweetness and the peace of real content.

H

THE FRIENDSHIP BOOK

SUNDAY—OCTOBER 17.

HEAVEN and earth will pass away, but my words shall not pass away.

MONDAY—OCTOBER 18.

MY friend, Jack McKibbin, of Dundonald, Belfast, enjoys a story with a smile.

Here's one about a neighbour's wee boy, aged six, who was at a party. He'd been well-warned to be on his best behaviour—and especially not to ask for second helpings.

When he arrived home his mother conducted the usual post-mortem. Ian assured his mother he had behaved perfectly.

" And did you ask for any second helpings?" his mother asked anxiously.

" No," replied Ian innocently. " I just took two helpings of everything the first time."

TUESDAY—OCTOBER 19.

ON the office desk of a certain successful business man is a toy doll—a mannikin, which bounces up however often it is knocked over. Its owner says that when he purchased it, it cost him nearly all he had.

The insistent way in which the little man bobs up after each knock has been a lifelong lesson to the business man, who attributes whatever success he has attained to his endeavours to live up to the principle the mannikin seems to embody:

" Down? Well, what of that?" it seems to say. " Every one gets knocked down now and then. What really counts is *what you do when you're down:* whether you *stay down,* or whether you refuse to stay there. Look at me—do as I do—jump up, and be at it again!"

WEDNESDAY—OCTOBER 20.

SOME years ago a nurse at a hospital was sorting out the locker of an old lady who had died in the geriatric ward. She found this remarkable poem in the old body's writing :

"What do you see, nurses, what do you see? What are you thinking when looking at me? A sulky old woman, not very wise, uncertain of habit, with far-away eyes ; who seems not to notice the things that you do, and for ever is losing a stocking or shoe?

"But inside me whiles a young girl still dwells, and now and again my battered heart swells ; I remember the joys, I remember the pain, and I'm living and loving life over again. So open your eyes, nurses, open and see, not a sulky old woman ; look closer—see ME."

Those lines deserve to be read and pondered over by all who deal, day by day, with old folk.

THURSDAY—OCTOBER 21.

JOHN WESLEY, the great evangelist who looked on the world as his parish, expected of others the same spirit of service and sacrifice of which he himself was such a shining example.

Once he showed his indignant anger with two brothers who, both bachelors, seemed to give so little to the church and its mission. He rebuked them, and they remained silent under his censure until he had finished. Then one explained, " A member of the church has got deeply into debt, and my brother and I live on a pennyworth of parsnips a day in order to pay off his debts and set him on his feet again."

John Wesley never again condemned anyone before learning all the circumstances.

THE FRIENDSHIP BOOK

WHAT'S the value of ten cigarettes and an ounce of tobacco?

To Bert Mann of Callander, they're worth more than words can tell. When Bert and his school-friend, Bob Leslie, of East Linton, marched off with the Royal Scots to the First World War, they went with a smile and a spring in their step.

But not long after, the tragedy of war was brought home to Bert in a terrible way. Bob, his boyhood chum, was killed by his side, and it fell to him to dig his grave on the battlefield of Flanders.

That Christmas, Bert was given a little brass box with ten cigarettes and an ounce of tobacco, a gift from Queen Alexandra to every serving soldier in the field. There and then, Bert vowed that he would keep his intact for all time, a keepsake of these years of sacrifice.

So, today, Bert will show you that little brass box with pride and sadness. For this old soldier, now over 80, it speaks of sorrow too deep for words, courage too splendid for medals, and memories too precious to share.

IT happened quite some time ago,
But caused you bitter pain,
Such anguish that you feel you can't
Trust anyone again.
But if you do, then you will find
Fresh joy of heart, new peace of mind.

CREATE in me a clean heart, O God; and renew a right spirit within me.

MONDAY—OCTOBER 25.

I KNOW a lonely old woman, soured and embittered, who will never see her son or grandchildren again.

I know a successful business man who hasn't a real friend in the world.

I know of a thousand sad and silly quarrels that will never be patched up. And all because someone is too proud to say " sorry."

To them, and to all, I pass on this advice :

An apology is a friendship preserver,
Is often a debt of honour,
Is never a sign of weakness,
Is an antidote for hatred,
Costs nothing but one's pride,
And always saves far, far more than it
    ever costs.

TUESDAY—OCTOBER 26.

ABOUT 17 years ago Alfred Hull of Luton planted an apple pip. It took root and grew and in 1963 one apple appeared which he gave to his daughter, Pamela.

The next year the tree bore 22 lb. of apples, all crisp, juicy and golden. But, tragically, by this time Pamela had died of cancer.

To find out what species of apple he was growing, Mr Hull sent samples to the Royal Horticultural Society. After many tests, they told him that somehow he had developed a new apple which was so good that it could be developed commercially. Mr Hull was asked to choose a name for it.

He remembered that first apple, and told them he wanted it to be called " Pam's Delight." And so Alfred Hull's apples will be an everlasting memorial to the daughter he loved.

WEDNESDAY—OCTOBER 27.

BARGEDDIE, on the outskirts of Glasgow, wants to say "thank you." Not to a beloved doctor, minister or schoolmaster, but to a retired miner named Neilie Brown, who lived by himself in a humble home in Dykehead Road.

Neilie became a helping hand to everybody. He went round the village every morning, knocking on doors and waking people for their work. Then round he went again with everybody's morning paper. When it came to pension day, he turned up at the post office, not only with his own book, but a whole bundle of others belonging to old folk who couldn't venture out themselves.

Each week at the bank he exchanged part of his pension for a pocketful of single shillings. Why? Because he knew people would be sure to need them over the week-end for their gas and electric meters! Soon, of course, everyone got to know about Neilie's store of shillings and many a thankful housewife blessed him for saving the Sunday dinner.

Neilie died in his seventies and is missed far more than he would ever have realised, as much for his friendly smile as for his helping hand. As I pass on this tribute on behalf of all Bargeddie, I commend the message it holds for you and me.

THURSDAY—OCTOBER 28.

A LITTLE girl and her father were walking along in the evening. She was fascinated by the stars, and kept looking up at them, but made no comment until her father asked what she was thinking. She replied, " If the bottom side of heaven is so beautiful, how wonderful the *other* side must be."

FRIDAY—OCTOBER 29.

IT'S five o'clock, the tea's not made,
   And Tom will soon be in;
The kids to bath, the room's a mess—
   I'm in a proper spin.
Then on the path I hear his step,
   His key turns in the door—
A smile, a kiss, a loving arm,
   And all seems bright once more.

SATURDAY—OCTOBER 30.

THERE was a wry smile from the Lady of the House at one of the letters that came out of my postbag.

It was from Mrs Beatrice Chapman, of Edmonton, Alberta, to thank me for the enjoyment she finds in my stories. " But," she adds, " one thing puzzles me. You often speak of the Lady of the House. Do you refer to your wife? Or is she the landlady where you board?"

I'd to chuckle at that. And, as I say, when I showed it to my wife she smiled, too. But I think we each knew what was in the other's mind—that too often, perhaps, a man's home becomes just somewhere to board; because, for some reason, to him other things have become more important than his wife and family ; and, without either of them realising it, husband and wife have slowly drifted apart over the years, instead of growing closer together.

It can happen so easily, too.

SUNDAY—OCTOBER 31.

GOD is our refuge and strength, a very present help in trouble.

NOVEMBER

MONDAY—NOVEMBER 1.

IT is to Spring Rice, American ambassador to the
Court of St James, London, we owe the
splendid lines :

There is another country I have heard of long ago
Most dear to them who love her and great to them
that know;
You cannot count her armies and you cannot see her
King,
Her fortress is a faithful heart and her pride is
suffering.
And one by one and silently her shining bounds
increase,
Her ways are ways of pleasantness and all her paths
are peace.

TUESDAY—NOVEMBER 2.

ROY SUTHERLAND, of Newbattle, near Edinburgh, collects children's sayings.

Recently, a friend of his was away for a few days.
Every night he phoned home for a word with his
wife and children. Lorna, who's six, answered one
evening. Just before handing the phone to her
mother, she told him, " Mummy loves you, and
Ian loves you, and Fiona loves you."

Daddy was touched, though he tried not to
show it. " But what about you, Lorna?" he teased.
" Don't you love me, too?"

There was a moment's silence. Then a small
voice said, " I thought you knew that, Daddy—
that's why I didn't bother to tell you."

D'you wonder that Daddy is firmly and for ever
wrapped around Lorna's little finger?

WEDNESDAY—NOVEMBER 3.

IF you are sorry for yourself,
  And life seems burdensome,
Don't sit around just feeling sad
Or hurt, or grieved, or glum.
Like birds that carol in the rain,
  Please sing a song or two.
You don't FEEL glad? Say, that's too bad—
  Just sing until you do!

THURSDAY—NOVEMBER 4.

EVER heard of David Brewster?

No reason why you should, I suppose. I only came across his name myself, by pure chance. He was born nearly two hundred years ago, son of the headmaster in Jedburgh, Roxburghshire. His mother died when he was only nine, and he was brought up by an older sister.

David's father was a severe man, and his childhood was not as happy as it might have been. Yet he shone at school, became a minister, then gave up the Church to study science. He did valuable work on colour blindness. He was fascinated by light, and helped design new lenses for lighthouses. He was knighted and became principal of St Andrews University, then vice-chancellor of Edinburgh University.

But what intrigues me is that he also invented the kaleidoscope—that long tube of cardboard, glass and mirrors into which generations of children, and their parents, have peered and gasped with delight at the millions of coloured patterns and designs which appear as the toy is shaken.

David died at 87, honoured by king and country. But I'm sure he must have been just as proud of the countless pleasure his magic box brought to a child.

THE FRIENDSHIP BOOK

WOMEN are different!

That may seem a fairly obvious thing to say, but the more you have to do with them the more you realise how different they are! This was brought home to me last week in a letter from Tom Slaven, of Gosforth.

Tom's home was burgled just before Christmas. It was a very distressing and cruel experience, as anyone who's been through the ordeal knows. As Tom rang the police, his wife sat down on the stairs and cried bitterly.

When he put down the receiver he tried his best to comfort her. " Don't be too upset, dear," he said soothingly. " After all, it can happen to anyone." His wife shook her head. " I'm not so upset about that," she replied.

Puzzled, Tom asked, " Then why are you crying?" His wife sniffed. " All my life," she said, " I've wanted to dial 999—and now *you've* gone and done it !"

Truly, as a mystified Tom Slaven declares, how little we men know about women !

START the day on the wrong side out,
Glum you'll end it, there's no doubt;
Smile at breakfast, there's a chance
All the day your heart will dance.
If by day your spirit's bright,
Chances are you'll sleep at night!

BEAR ye one another's burdens, and so fulfil the law of Christ.

THE FRIENDSHIP BOOK

MONDAY—NOVEMBER 8.

WHEN someone dear to us passes beyond our mortal knowledge, how often we may sigh, "I wish I had been kinder when she was alive." Our saddest regret is that the chance has gone for ever.

The great Samuel Johnson experienced that remorse. For, as a youth he had been too proud to serve in his father's booth at the market place at Lichfield when his parent was sick. It so preyed on his mind in later years that one day he stood for two hours bareheaded in the pouring rain on the site of the booth in penitent remorse.

Better the deed in life than the memory of neglect in death.

TUESDAY—NOVEMBER 9.

DO these lines give us a portrait of the modern granny?
Perhaps they do—and then, perhaps they don't!
The old rocking-chair will be empty today,
For Grandma no longer is in it.
She's off in her car to her office or shop—
She buzzes around every minute.
You won't see her trundling off early to bed
From her chair in a warm chimney nook,
Her typewriter's clicking far into the night,
Because Grandma is writing a book!
Our heroine never allows backward looks
To slow down her steady advancing.
There's no baby-sitting for her any more—
For Grandma has taken up dancing.
She isn't content with her thoughts of old times,
With meagre and second-hand knowledge.
So don't bring your mending for Grandma to do,
For Grandma has gone back to college!

THE FRIENDSHIP BOOK

WHILE visiting a friend in Killearn, Stirlingshire, the Lady of the House suggested we go to see the salmon leaping up the river a few miles away. So we walked in the sunshine past a little white cottage, and down the steps leading to the River Endrick and the famous waterfall that goes into the deep pool known as the Pots of Gartness.

What an incredible sight! A torrent of water thundering down, boiling with foam and spray, and the salmon leaping towards the narrow channel, six feet or more above them, that allows them to swim upriver.

We saw fish of every size hurling themselves up the solid wall of water that bore down on them. All with one object — to climb the waterfall. It seemed impossible. Time and again they were flung back into the pool below. One fish made twenty-five attempts before it succeeded. Spellbound, we watched in silence for nearly an hour before, reluctantly, we turned to go.

Yet the memory remains and, with it, a parable. This country of ours, too, goes forward to meet great odds. Much is against us. Yet, like the salmon of Gartness, if each of us were to strive against these odds, to see every setback as a challenge, and to deny the possibility of failure, who can doubt we, too, would reach our goal?

TWO minutes in a whole, round year—
A trifling time to give
To brave and battle-weary men,
Who died that we might live.
Aye, long ago it was—and yet
Who now among us dare forget?

FRIDAY—NOVEMBER 12.

A FRIEND of mine is a poultry farmer just outside town.

Often, children come to his door for eggs for their mothers. Usually they're able to say what size they want—large, standard, medium, &c. But one youngster who turned up last week simply looked mystified when the farmer's wife asked what kind he'd come for.

Then his face cleared, and, confidently, he replied, " It's ones for boiling, missus !"

SATURDAY—NOVEMBER 13.

WHAT'S the matter with Mrs Craig?

For 1040 Sundays she never missed the morning service in her church. She's had a perfect record of attendance for 20 years.

How did she manage that?

Doesn't Mrs Craig ever have people coming to see her on Sundays, so she's too busy for church?

Doesn't she ever go anywhere on Saturday night, so she's too tired on Sunday morning?

Doesn't she ever have headaches, colds, nervous spells, tummy upsets on Sundays?

Doesn't she ever sleep late on Sunday morning?

Doesn't she have any friends who invite her away for the week-end?

Doesn't it ever rain or snow in her town?

Don't the buses ever break down, and doesn't she ever miss them?

Doesn't someone at the church ever hurt her feelings?

Doesn't she ever become angry at the minister?

Doesn't she have a garden that needs weeded, a car that needs washed, a lunch that needs cooked?

What on earth is the matter with Mrs Craig . . .?

SUNDAY—NOVEMBER 14.

NO poppies grow in English fields
At this time of the year,
Though poppies bloom in every street—
Like magic they appear.
For we who live are proud to give
A sigh for all who died,
And brought us loneliness and grief,
Yet filled our hearts with pride . . .
Those gallant ones who fought and fell,
Remember well . . . remember well.

MONDAY—NOVEMBER 15.

A KHAKI-clad young soldier was relating some of his experiences during the Great War.

" They took me from my home and put me in barracks ; they took away my clothes and put me in khaki ; they took away my name and gave me a number. They took me to church where I'd never been before, and they made me listen to a sermon for 40 minutes. Then the parson said, ' No. 575—Art thou weary, art thou languid?'—and I got seven days' C.B. for giving him a civil answer !"

TUESDAY—NOVEMBER 16.

OLD WILLIE, a retired fisherman, lived down by the harbour at Cellardyke.

The new minister was visiting in the neighbourhood and gave Willie a call. After chatting of this and that, the minister rose to go.

"Well, well, Mr Mathews," said Willie, " any time you're down by the harbour, see an' drop in !"

On reflection, the minister hoped he didn't mean what he said.

SERENITY

The rainbow tells, however dark the cloud,
The sun soon shines in glory once again,
And in its rays a church tower, gleaming proud,
Brings hope in darkest hours to hearts of men.

DAVID HOPE

THE RIVER

The rushing roaring waters
Crash loudly on their way,
Showering rocks and bushes
With clouds of foaming spray,

But once this mighty torrent,
  Though unlikely it may seem,
Was a trickle in the heather,
  A little mountain stream.

DAVID HOPE

WINTER JOY

If we never had snow
We never would know
The gifts of a winter's day:
There's joy and good health
And a world of wealth
Waiting along the way.

DAVID HOPE

WEDNESDAY—NOVEMBER 17.

I FOUND a faded snap today
Of Jim and me, just wed;
It made me cry — I know not why!
I should have smiled instead.
And yet the memories it brought
Gave me the courage which I sought.

THURSDAY—NOVEMBER 18.

JIM ROBERTSON, a friend in Clydebank, is a keen angler and has a fund of fishing yarns.

He tells the story of the man who, after a day fishing on Loch Leven, hooked a beauty—a three-pounder. Bursting with pride, he carried his trout to where his friend was standing with his own catch—five tiddlers, not one over half a pound.

He laid his fish down beside them and waited for a comment. His friend regarded it impassively for a few moments, looked at his own catch, then back again at the big one.

" Ah, yes, Bill," he said calmly. " So you just caught the one, then?"

FRIDAY—NOVEMBER 19.

HOW many of us may never get going because we can't make up our minds. I was reminded of this when I came across these lines :

" *A centipede was happy quite*
Until a frog in fun
Said, ' Pray, which leg comes after which?'
This raised her mind to such a pitch
She lay distracted in the ditch
Considering how to run."

Today's decision becomes tomorrow's venture.

THE FRIENDSHIP BOOK

I'D like to tell you a story of the February election in 1974.

We were in the grip of a fuel crisis. There was no heating in many polling stations, including the one in the Border village of Smailholm.

Well, one of the first to vote there was a retired roadman, Robbie Robertson. He saw the girls on duty were frozen, and ten minutes later he was back carrying a tray with cups, saucers, a big pot of tea, milk, sugar and a plate of buttered Selkirk bannocks from his cottage. " Just something to warm you up, lassies," he smiled. And for the rest of the day, until polling ended at ten that night, Robbie kept coming in every hour or two with more tea and scones. When the official voting was over, there was a vote of thanks for Robbie the roadman.

In the October election, the one man the girls were looking out for was Robbie. He didn't appear, and they learned that he had died a few weeks before, at 75. They found, too, that he'd spent his life helping others—digging gardens, going errands for the old and ill, clearing paths of snow, giving away fruit, flowers and vegetables from his garden.

Indeed, the funeral of the old roadman was the biggest Smailholm had ever known, with teachers, doctors, businessmen and farmers from far afield joining the village in honouring one who, in every way, made life's road easier for others.

BE of good comfort, be of one mind, live in peace : and the God of love and peace shall be with you.

THE FRIENDSHIP BOOK

I DON'T know who the singing joiner of Dundee is, but he was sent to fix up a special handrail for Mrs Reilly's husband. You see, he has multiple sclerosis, and on the day the joiner came he was in bed, feeling low and depressed.

The moment the joiner stepped through the door and opened up his tool-kit he began to sing. He sang as he fitted the rail and screwed in the nails. He sang as he tidied up and put his tools away—popular songs, ballads, the latest from the Top Twenty, and so on. His voice filled the house. It echoed through the lobby and the landing and into every room.

It brightened the kitchen where Mrs Reilly was working. It lit up the bedroom where the crippled man lay, making him smile. Indeed, Mrs Reilly says her husband has been a different man since the singing joiner came—and she asked me to say a special thank you to him.

I do so gladly, ma'am.

"**I**T'S more blessed to give than to receive."

But it's also true to say that some ways of receiving are more blessed than others!

When the harvest thanksgiving gifts were being distributed from one church, two women received a big bag of apples. The first said, " What on earth were you thinking about? I can't use these !"

The other beamed with delight. " With me not being able to get out and about, I'll be able to give these to the children who run errands for me."

God loveth a cheerful giver—and I'm pretty sure that he has a soft spot for a grateful receiver, too !

WEDNESDAY—NOVEMBER 24.

ONE of the best-known incidents in English history is the story of Sir Walter Raleigh, and how he spread his costly cloak on the ground that Queen Elizabeth might walk over it and keep her shoes from being soiled.

It is a pretty story and evidence of a courtly heart. But it has a humble life counterpart in the early years of this century.

Miss Ellen Terry, the great actress, was to perform in a theatre somewhere in a Scottish town. The night was a wet one, and the streets were muddy. When her carriage drew up to the doors of the theatre, a poor newspaper boy, seeing that she would have to wade across the muddy pavement, placed one or two of his papers on the ground that the great actress might walk across them and not get her shoes soiled or her feet wet.

After the incident, she wrote a letter to this lad, which he cherished to his dying day, thanking him for the sweet and lovely act that he had performed.

It reminds us of the words of Tennyson :
" *For manners are not idle, but the fruit*
Of loyal natures and of noble minds."

THURSDAY—NOVEMBER 25.

WHEN gazing backwards down the miles you've
tramped along life's road,
Think not just of their weariness, nor of your heavy
load;
But that, though shadows darkened oft your path and
made it grey,
The sunshine brightened many miles of life's long, uphill
way.

FRIDAY—NOVEMBER 26.

I THINK I know Chrissie Ritchie's secret!

Chrissie, a widow in her 70's, lives alone. Her home is never empty, for people enjoy going to see her—not only old friends but young ones, too. Children, from round about, young mothers, too, find a welcome, a friendly ear, and wise advice. Teenagers, who once came from the youth club to paint her kitchen, keep coming back.

What's her secret? Part of it, I'm sure, is printed on a card fixed to the frame of her kitchen window with a drawing pin, just above the sink. There are four simple lines on it :

I try to watch the words I say,
I keep them soft and sweet—
For I never know, from day to day,
Which ones I'll have to eat!

SATURDAY—NOVEMBER 27.

WHAT'S in a name?

Miss R. M. MacFadyen, Manchester, told me of a teacher friend who was filling out a form giving details of her new class of five-year-olds. " What's your father's name, Donald?" she asked one little lad. " I don't know," he replied. Again she tried. " Is it Donald, same as yours?" she prompted. Once more the wee chap shook his head.

So the teacher made a last desperate attempt. " Well," she smiled, " what does your mother call your father?"

Donald's chin went up. " She doesn't call him anything," he retorted. " She *likes* him !"

SUNDAY—NOVEMBER 28.

WE are all one in Christ Jesus.

THE FRIENDSHIP BOOK

MONDAY—NOVEMBER 29.

HERE'S something to smile at and think about. It was said years ago by the great American comedian, Will Rogers. But, like so many of Will's words, there is more than a touch of down-to-earth commonsense there, too.

" Even if you're on the right track," said Will, " you'll get run over if you just sit there !"

TUESDAY—NOVEMBER 30

JESSIE TAIT, over 70, came from Ireland to visit a friend in Manchester.

When she arrived she was taken ill and had to go into hospital. The friend with whom she'd planned to spend a few days was going off to Canada. So Jessie didn't know what to do when the doctors told her that, although she could leave hospital, she'd have to come back as an out-patient for a few weeks. She knew no one in Manchester with whom she could stay.

Iris-Ann, the young lass in the next bed, smiled across. " Never mind, Gran," she said kindly, " you can come and stay with me until you're better." And, sure enough, Iris-Ann took Jessie into her home and looked after her for a month. And Jean, one of Iris-Ann's friends, borrowed a small van to take Jessie to hospital for her treatment, and to give her a wee run now and again.

Jessie's holiday didn't turn out quite as she expected. But she has made friends she'll never forget, and whose kindness she'll never be able to repay.

I don't suppose that when Iris-Ann next hears the parable of the good Samaritan, she'll think of herself. But how splendidly she has lived up to its challenge.

DECEMBER

THINGS aren't always what they seem. The thought is brought to mind by this letter from an Arbroath housewife.

" Dear Francis, I'm an ordinary housewife who promised a neighbour I'd get some odds and ends for her in the supermarket. I put my own purchases in the store's basket, and my neighbour's into my own shopping bag.

" All went well until I reached the check-out. There were stares from all around. The staff who'd gathered there were nudging and whispering to each other. I suddenly realised they thought I was a shoplifter, trying to steal the items in my shopping bag ! As I took them out one by one, I blushed crimson, like a guilty schoolgirl. Stupidly, I never dreamed of what people might think. And when I tried to explain—oh, dear ! You should just have heard the knowing comments !

" I still feel, every time I go into that store, that I'm being given the eagle eye."

Don't be *too* hasty to judge . . .

IT'S a dirty old town I've heard people say, but wanderers returning their true thoughts betray; they may leave with pleasure and far may they roam, but there's no truer saying, there's no place like home.

The place of your birth remains dear to your heart, it's the one special corner on earth set apart, the streets of heart's memory are still paved with gold, recalling the joys that will never grow old.

FRIDAY—DECEMBER 3.

THOMAS A KEMPIS, who achieved fame through writing his " Life of Christ," once invited a young monk to go into the town to preach. Together they visited the market-place, talked with the stall-holders, strolled through the streets and saluted those they met, falling into conversation with any passers-by who stopped to greet them.

When they returned to the monastery the disappointed youth protested, " Brother Thomas, we spent all that time in the town and not once did we preach."

" On the contrary," pointed out the older monk, " wherever we went we were noted of men and judged by our manner, our bearing and our conversation, and so we were preaching all the time."

A man himself may be his own best sermon.

SATURDAY—DECEMBER 4.

I MUST admit I often take our milkman for granted, and I expect most people do.

Mrs Imrie, of Stockport, tells me she has never taken her milkman for granted since the occasion when, some years ago, she'd found a burst pipe in her kitchen and was struggling to stop the water flow when her milkman came to her rescue. " How can I repay you ?" she asked, wondering if she should look for her purse.

She tells me his answer, given with a smile, stopped her in her tracks. " You can't repay a good turn. You accept it—and pass it on. That way one good turn becomes a link in a never-ending chain."

Mrs Imrie has never forgotten her milkman's advice. I don't think I will, either.

THE FRIENDSHIP BOOK

SUNDAY—DECEMBER 5.

MASTERS, give unto your servants that which is just and equal; knowing that ye also have a Master in heaven.

MONDAY—DECEMBER 6.

DO not, I beg, despair today
When deep and sudden grief
Has come to shock and frighten you,
Almost beyond belief.
Pause yet a little. Bravely wait.
God's grace to comfort you is great.

TUESDAY—DECEMBER 7.

ONE day a village organist was practising on his church organ. He was playing a piece by Mendelssohn, and was not playing it very well.

A stranger sat in the back pew of the church. He heard the organist playing the music and, when he had finished, asked if he would allow him to play. "Certainly not," said the organist, gruffly. "I never allow anyone to touch the organ but myself." "I would be glad if you would allow me the privilege." Again the organist gave a gruff refusal. After the third request, the appeal was granted, although very ungraciously.

The stranger sat at the organ, pulled out the stops and began to play the same piece. But what a change! It was as though the church was filled with music from Heaven.

Afterwards, the organist asked the stranger, "Who are you?"

You can imagine his feelings when the stranger told him he was Mendelssohn. The two parted the best of friends.

THE FRIENDSHIP BOOK

WEDNESDAY—DECEMBER 8.

HARRY S. TRUMAN, former President of the United States, was a modest man and quite a fount of home-spun philosophy. Talking about the Presidency, he said, " I was there more or less by accident you might say, and I just never got to thinking I was anything *special*. I tried never to forget who I was and where I'd come from and where I was going back to. And if you can do that, things usually work out all right in the end."

When Harry gave up the great office of Presidency, he and his wife, Bess, took the train back home to Independence, Missouri. Later, a TV reporter asked the ex-President what was the first thing he did when he got home.

He got the simple reply : " I carried the grips (suitcases) up to the attic."

THURSDAY—DECEMBER 9.

AN inquiring little boy had asked his mother what it was to be wise, and so she sent him to a wise man who lived nearby, to ask from him the secret of his wisdom.

" Listen," said the old man.

The little boy sat down and waited for more. But there was no more to come. The crux of the man's wisdom lay in that one little word—LISTEN.

FRIDAY—DECEMBER 10.

SURE, quite a lot is wrong, yet it
Is really no excuse
For grumbling and for looking glum,
Declaring life's no use.
Now and again, just try a smile —
You might find life much more worthwhile!

THE FRIENDSHIP BOOK

DR ALBERT SCHWEITZER was talking to students on his favourite theme, reverence for life. He explained that he had had no time to learn English and so he would speak in French. A shaft of sunlight caught his white hairs and he glowed as he urged upon them this reverence for life, for all creatures, for the tiniest, " la plus petite." Looking at their chairs he pointed out that they could break one of those chairs, solid as they were, and put it together again, with care and patience; but " break a fly, the tiniest of creatures," and no amount of human skill, effort or ingenuity could put it together again.

His enthusiasm transformed the well-made chairs into dull, lifeless things, while the bluebottle on the window, picked out by the sunbeam, shone a more vivid blue and buzzed more loudly. It became the thing of value.

ABHOR that which is evil; cleave to that which is good.

ISN'T this world a wonderful place ? Consider these facts : If all the oceans of the world were massed together on one side, no human life would be possible; if the air was more or less than it is no human life would be possible; and if the gravitational pull were more or less than it actually is, we would either be stuck to the earth or we would float.

The seas, the air and the force of gravity are all just right. The Creator's hand never falters.

THE FRIENDSHIP BOOK

SOME of my friends have a gift for seeing happy truths in everyday life. An old acquaintance was delighted by an incident when visiting a friend in hospital.

Farther up the ward, a patient who'd had an eye operation was lying disconsolately, his head swathed in bandages, when down the ward strode a beautiful nurse with a glorious coffee-coloured skin. She carried a bowl of soup to the blind man's bed. She propped him up, then with many laughs, in a voice rich as the sunshine from her home country, she helped him eat in what were obviously his first fumbling attempts to cope with blindness.

It'll be a long time before my friend forgets this simple example of what nursing is all about. Cheerfulness, comfort and help. But, just as important, that blindness sees no colour bar !

WEDNESDAY—DECEMBER 15.

I SUPPOSE it's inevitable our lives should be ruled by the clock.

I was speaking to a primary teacher who'd asked her class to write a story on " Why I like my grandma." There were many touching tributes. But one wee lad's made the teacher think :

" I like my grandma because she doesn't have a watch . . ."

When he asks her to tell him a story, she doesn't look at the time and say, " Well, just a short one." When they go out for a walk, she doesn't say, " We'll have to hurry home for tea." When he goes round to see her, she doesn't say, " I'm going out in five minutes."

Grandma doesn't have a watch. She has something far more precious : All the time in the world.

THE FRIENDSHIP BOOK

A VISITOR to Long Island, New York, was interested to see so many pools of water on the island, some big and others quite small. But what puzzled him was that some of the pools had clear water and smelled sweet while others were murky and sour.

He understood why when he was told that many of the pools were open to the sea and washed by the tide twice a day; the others were landlocked and had no outlet.

Queen Victoria once complained to Gladstone, " Why, sir, are there so many nasty and sour grown-ups when all the babies are so sweet and lovely ?"

Isn't the answer simply that some of us grow to be self-centred and inward-looking while some open their lives to others in service and love ?

IN his enforced exile abroad owing to ill-health, Robert Louis Stevenson often found his memory travelling home to Scotland. One of his poems is about Leerie, the lamplighter, lighting the lamps in the dusk of Edinburgh.

Lights had a fascination for him as a child and he recalled often his pleasure and delight when, unable to sleep because of his hacking cough, his nannie in his home at Herriot Row would lift him out of bed to see the lighted windows in the terraces of the New Town stretching up to Princes Street. It comforted him to know that there were others who could not sleep in the silent watches of the night.

However lonely we may feel, we are *never* alone— not even in sickness and sorrow.

SATURDAY—DECEMBER 18.

I'VE never pretended to be a golfer.

But I can sympathise with the visitor to St Andrews who all his life had dreamed of playing a round on the famous Old Course and made a hash of almost every stroke.

Thoroughly demoralised, he and his caddie trailed disconsolately off the eighteenth green. As he tipped the caddie he commented sadly, " There can't be many worse golfers than me."

The caddie patted his arm. " Well, well, maybe there are," he said. " But they dinna play !"

SUNDAY—DECEMBER 19.

BRETHREN, let us love one another, for love is of God.

MONDAY—DECEMBER 20.

WHEN Jane, who's four, paid one of her regular calls on the Lady of the House the other day, I thought I'd better admire the colourful sticker on her jumper.

" Oh, that," said Jane, not too happily. " I got 't from Alice and Ann's mummy. She got five with her shopping, and Alice and Ann got two and I got one."

" Gosh, weren't you lucky," I said a trifle heartily. And I knew from the way Jane looked at me I'd gone wrong somewhere.

" No," she said seriously. " If you got one, that was fair. You were lucky if you got two."

Well, it's easy to smile at Jane's philosophy of life, and I had a hard job not to at the time, but afterwards I couldn't help wondering if maybe too many of us think we're " entitled " to a bit too much.

THE FRIENDSHIP BOOK

UNABLE to see a way out of their despair, some
people are tempted to end their life.

Some years ago, Mrs Knighton of Preston was
discharged from hospital as a semi-invalid, unable
to walk without agony. What a burden to her
family, she told herself. They'd be far better off
without her. So early next morning she decided to
gas herself as soon as her husband and children
had gone. Before her husband left, he brought the
morning paper to her bedroom and she said good-bye
to him for the last time. Turning over the pages
she saw it was Derby Day. Across the back page
were these words : NEVER SAY DIE. Of course
it was the name of one of the horses in the race.
But for Mrs Knighton it was like a message from
beyond. She broke down and wept, forgetting her
thoughts of suicide.

From that day her health improved steadily and
she found that life was all she ever hoped it might be.

Never Say Die ! Could any message be clearer
to those who know despair ?

MANY people seem to think that you have to
know a lot of complicated etiquette to have
good manners. But it's really much simpler than
that. In Bernard Shaw's " Pygmalion," Professor
Higgins explains :

" The great secret, Eliza, is not having bad
manners or good manners or any other particular
sort of manners, but having the same manner for
all human souls ; in short, behaving as if you were
in heaven, where there are no third-class carriages
and one soul is as good as another."

That's all there is to it.

THE FRIENDSHIP BOOK

IT'S comforting when trouble comes
To share it with a friend;
To talk it over, bit by bit,
With someone who will spend
A while with you until you see
More clearly what to do,
And strength and courage for the task
Are somehow given you.
Yes, trouble seems less hard to bear
If someone will your burden share.

FRIDAY—DECEMBER 24.

THOMAS TELFORD, the renowned engineer, had not slept for some nights. The first huge chain of his immense suspension bridge linking Anglesey to Wales across the Menai Straits was about to be hauled into position. No one had built such a bridge before, and five years had gone into the construction of the great foundations, arches and towers.

At last all was ready, and 150 labourers began the slow winding of the capstans until the chain was drawn to the top of the tower. A great cheer rose from the multitude of sightseers, and the National Anthem was struck up.

At the end of all the celebration and festivity, somebody noticed that Telford himself was missing. He was found on his knees, thanking God that everything had been achieved without harm to a single person.

Telford's magnificent bridge across the Menai Straits was opened in 1826 and still stands, a hundred feet above high water. A lasting tribute to his imaginative vision and his concern for the safety of all who used his work.

THE FRIENDSHIP BOOK

I RECEIVED a Christmas card the other day with the following verses and thought you might like to share them with me:

In the fulness of time, in a faraway clime,
God sent down a Saviour to earth,
And the wise men were led by a star to His bed,
The herald which told of His birth.

It will lead us aright through the darkness of night,
To Jesus our Saviour and King
And our hearts once so sad, will rejoice and be glad,
He cometh — Salvation to bring!

AND the angel said unto them, Fear not: for, behold, I bring you good tidings of great joy, which shall be to all people.

IAN, whose parents live near us, is four.

He's a fine wee lad, but his father and mother are worried because he's such a bad loser. He hates being last—indeed, he's not happy unless he wins.

One day last week Ian was at a birthday party. He arrived home to say he'd been last at everything—yet he was beaming broadly. His father was proud that at last his son had learned to take failure like a man. Then Ian added, " And from now on I'm *always* going to be last."

Mystified, Dad asked why—and it turned out Ian was last at pass the parcel, and had been left holding the prize when the music stopped!

Truly, the last shall be first . . .

THE FRIENDSHIP BOOK

"WHEN you're young," a doctor friend remarked recently, " it is impossible to understand what it means to be old.

" I remember," he went on, " being irritated at my grandfather who always took a stick when he went out. It was so silly—he could stride around his garden without it quite happily.

" Only recently," he said, " did I realise that when you are old your eyes can play dangerous tricks with you. Although you can move around safely in your own garden, you're not so sure of yourself on a pavement half a mile from home."

He added that his mother, whose hands trembled at sixty, pretended she did not like tea, or that it was not good for her, simply because she was much too proud to pick up a cup of hot tea when friends were present—to have spilled it in company would have been unthinkable !

Yes, growing old brings its embarrassments . . . and perhaps, by understanding a little better we may be a little more gentle.

BEFORE Abraham Lincoln became the President of the United States he was riding with some friends across the prairie and through the woods. As they passed under a tree they noticed a little bird which had fallen from its nest. They all passed, but all at once Lincoln turned back and helped it back to its nest.

His friends waited for him, saw what he did, and asked him afterwards why he had troubled to go back for such a small thing as that.

Lincoln replied, " I can only say this—I feel the better for it."

THE FRIENDSHIP BOOK

A HOTEL manager friend of mine told me this story about a young girl who had just come over from Malta to work for him as a chambermaid.

She woke one morning to find a white carpet of snow covering the hotel grounds. She'd never seen snow in her life before and was so thrilled that what do you think she did? She rushed right out in her nightdress and put a little bit in an envelope to send home to her family!

As my friend said, it takes a fresh eye to make us realise how we take the miracles of nature for granted.

I DON'T suppose you've ever heard of Teen Miller, who died in Dundee at the age of 92. As many of her friends as could manage went along to St Paul's Cathedral to bid her farewell.

Teen Miller's home was a tenement and almost all her life was spent working in a jute mill. She began as a girl of nine. And for no fewer than 74 years, she had been content to do a humble job as well as she could. She lived a good and simple life, with always something to give to her church, and she found her great rewards in her friends, her family and her faith.

Now I'm not saying the secret of happiness is to work in a jute mill, or anywhere else, for 74 years. But I do say that, in the way Teen lived her life, there's a lesson for us all. You can aim high without wishing for the moon. You can value the things you possess higher than those you'd like to possess. You can earn a contentment that money cannot buy.

Teen Miller knew that, and as she was borne from the cathedral to the sound of the great organ, I think her friends knew it, too.

K

Where the Photographs were taken

FROST FLOWERS — *Worcester.*

THOUGHTS — *Hope Cove, Devon.*

CHANGE — *Harlech Castle, Merionethshire.*

SAFE HAVEN — *Aberdour, Fife.*

AT PEACE — *Cambridge.*

WELCOME — *River Exe.*

JOY OF LIFE — *Cumberland.*

LUCKY PEOPLE — *Swan Green, New Forest, Hampshire.*

LONDON TULIPS — *Parliament Square, London.*

HOLIDAY MAGIC — *Mousehole, Cornwall.*

CONTENT — *Bran End, Essex.*

LONE PINE TREE — *Shieldaig, Ross-shire.*

PERFECTION — *Sonning Lock, Berkshire.*

TIMELESS — *Shipley Church, Sussex.*

LOOKING UPWARDS — *Clifden, Connemara, Co. Galway.*

PASSING HOURS — *Abinger Hammer, Surrey.*

THE SKETCHERS — *Salisbury Cathedral, Wiltshire.*

SERENITY — *Newbury, Berkshire.*

THE RIVER — *River Dochart at Killin, Perthshire.*

Printed and Published by D. C. THOMSON & Co., LTD.
185 Fleet Street, London EC4A 2HS.
© D. C. Thomson & Co , Ltd., 1975.